A LIFE DESCRIBES A BOOK

DESCRIBES A LIFE

AHSAHTA PRESS

BOISE, IDAHO
2012

THE NEW SERIES
#49

WORK FROM MEMORY

IN RESPONSE TO
IN SEARCH OF LOST TIME
BY MARCEL PROUST

POETRY BY DAN BEACHY-QUICK
PROSE BY MATTHEW GOULISH

Ahsahta Press, Boise State University, Boise, Idaho 83725-1525
ahsahtapress.org
Cover design by Quemadura
Book design by Janet Holmes
Printed in Canada
Acknowledgments appear on p. 97.

LIBRARY OF CONGRESS CATALOGING-IN-PUBLICATION DATA

Beachy-Quick, Dan, 1973-
Work from memory : in response to In search of lost time by Marcel Proust :
poetry / by Dan Beachy-Quick ; prose by Matthew Goulish.
p. cm. — (The new series ; 49)
ISBN 978-1-934103-30-2 (PBK. : ALK. PAPER)
ISBN 1-934103-30-6 (PBK. : ALK. PAPER)
I. Goulish, Matthew, 1960- II. Title.
PS3602.E24W66 2012
811'.6—DC23
2012023444

CONTENTS

for Jean and Sol Radam

there was earth inside them, and / they dug

and for the Hixsons of Columbus, Ohio

PART 1

The neurology team's report introduces the patient KC post-accident, living with misalignments of memory. KC *suffered widespread brain damage that included almost complete hippocampal loss bilaterally following a closed-head injury twenty years ago. Qualitative assessment revealed remote memory loss that was minimal in duration for factual information but relatively complete for personal episodes. Consistent with the extent of his damage, he exhibited a severe anterograde and retrograde amnesia for autobiographical episodes associated with visually presented family photographs. There was no sign that the photographs triggered any feeling of re-experiencing or emotional response. KC was unable to place events in the photographs within a temporal-spatial context or relate them to any life experiences beyond that which was obvious to any individual seeing the photographs for the first time. Even after extensive prompting, he could not recreate an episode from any part of his life. This was in sharp contrast to his relatively preserved conceptual autobiographical knowledge and world knowledge, as indicated by his ability to identify the people within family photographs, as well as famous names and places, and to define words from time periods across his pre-morbid life span except for the 5–10 years before his accident. Similar to this pattern of personal and general semantic preservation but autobiographical episodic impairment, KC appears to have retained a schematic cognitive map sufficient for navigation in an environment experienced since he was 9 years old, but has lost more detailed topographical features of that environment, such as the appearance of salient houses.*

Current neurology attributes three forms of memory to the human brain: episodic, semantic, and procedural. Semantic memory connects words to stimuli. For this test, the team asked KC whether the upper case form of a letter involves only straight lines, a combination of straight and

A life describes a book describes a life
A poem cannot think when the candle burns out
Little wick this dark pronominal life distends
He is a child and I am falling asleep in the book

*

Page an enchanted preface to the night's dream
Ink the erotic other expands there is no self to think
Here is where I am never the same
Waking in the dark some body the same body as mine

*

There is no time but we live in time
We do not die but we die each of us all at once
Transparent plane I see through myself to see
The pane of glass red with the setting sun

curved lines, or only curved lines. The patient answered correctly for the letters K and M (straight); D, B, and P (combination); and C, Q, and G (curved, with the exception of tails on G and Q). Similarly, when a doctor asked KC whether the named animal possessed large or small ears, he a correctly replied for rabbit (large), donkey (large), and otter (small). Place name recognition also tests for semantic memory. The visual recognition test of the family photo album assesses episodic memory, or the ability to place oneself in one's memories and one's memories in a sequence. The re-navigation of an experienced environment relies on procedural memory—that which, for example, retains a skill such as bicycle riding. With primary damage to episodic memory, the patient can retain the lesson learned but not the memory of learning it. He can remember how to walk through his old neighborhood, differentiate streetlamps from trees, perhaps even name a hawthorn in bloom, but not recall his connection to any of these images, and thus fail to identify *the appearance of salient houses*. KC recalls his past, but not as a past that includes himself.

The report on KC influenced debates about animal perceptions of time. Does a western scrub-jay have a concept of *the future*? The scrub jay buries its food: a pinion nut in one spot and a grub in another. For five days it will prefer to dig up and eat the grub. On the sixth day it will dig up the nut. Does the jay live only in the present, making decisions based on smell? Or does it remember its food's location, and plan to dig it up "tomorrow"? The research of Nicola Clayton, through a series of detailed experiments, proposed that the scrub jay has a sense of time similar to our own, perhaps more acute. It appears not only to exhibit the semantic memory of orientation and the procedural memory of digging and burying, but also the episodic memory that KC lacks, placing itself and its food in a time continuum. The scrub jay inhabits a duration that begins with the double burial and ends in a doubly possible future. Furthermore, the jay appears to possess an internal clock that alerts it to the passing of five days. The last nut reappearance concludes the episode that began with grub and nut burial in the scrub jay's life.

What remains open for KC for the scrub jay is closed.

Child tormented by time that enchants
The dripping wax measuring the candle's length
A tear that is a condition
In his mother's kiss an abstracted vision

*

Every day another self places its thin glass
Pane over previous pane the same light
May or may not illuminate them all a soul
In every object waiting to be recognized to be

*

Released the aperture opens on the film
To be seen is to be accurate a camera defines
The eye as object seeing object the cathedral
Inverted the steeple points down

Books bookend the project of the book. They open it, and they close it.

Sometimes, my candle scarcely out, my eyes would close so quickly that I did not have time to say to myself: "I'm falling asleep." The first book, read and dreamed in a transparent state between waking and sleeping, resembles the book we are now reading, although virtual, as if the image of it finished composes a necessary step in the construction, the *initiation.* We glimpse the first book in a moment with the veil lifted, as the meeting of reality and potentiality, the realization that this is the book of the self—*it seemed to me that I myself was the immediate subject of the book: a church, a quartet, the rivalry between Francois I and Charles V*—not precisely the self who lives, but the self who is written. *This belief lived on for a few seconds after my waking; it did not shock my reason but lay heavy like scales on my eyes and kept them from realizing that the candlestick was no longer lit. Then it began to grow unintelligible to me, as after metempsychosis do the thoughts of an earlier existence; the subject of the book detached itself from me, I was free to apply myself to it or not; immediately I recovered my sight and I was amazed to find a darkness around me . . .* The writing self, who has yet to undertake the labor and the life, sees the written self already finished, illuminated to closed eyes with the light of memory, projected into the future, and named as such after the waking to darkness. *I would ask myself what time it might be; I could hear the whistling of the trains which, remote or near by, like the singing of a bird in a forest, plotting the distances, described to me the extent of the deserted countryside where the traveller hastens towards the nearest station; and the little road he is following will be engraved on his memory by the excitement he owes to new places, to unaccustomed activities, to the recent conversation and the farewells under the unfamiliar lamp that follow him still through the silence of the night, to the imminent sweetness of his return.*

The life and the writing blaze the trail through the aporia, the roadless nocturnal countryside. They navigate the immensity of the labor by landmarks new and old at once, by virtue of similarity. The train

Perception stops at the face *a puberty of grief*
Vision gilt on the surface a glittering other
Grammarless being the eye is an introduction
To a pinhole void light dilates into darker wonder

*

A dream figure birthed from a cramp in his thigh
The child thought he could think into her
Who was his thought before his mind could think it
Little beating mind a pulse sounds like a footprint

*

Before the foot has stepped onto the grass
Fate is in the face though the face denies it
The dream seems a promise it may or may not break
The future a phrase whose music repeats

echoes the bird. The lived life constructs and uncovers the written life as discovery and return, as to bury it now according to the perfect image of the day it will be recovered.

The second book at the end is the end. Unchanged from childhood, still in its place with its contents, it remains as remembered while overflowing memory. Its constancy throws us back to the first book which is now not transformed but re-revealed as having already contained the journey that was about to transpire. *As I entered the library where I had been pursuing this train of thought . . . without paying very much attention to what I was doing, I had been taking first one and then another of the precious volumes from the shelves, when suddenly, at the moment when I carelessly opened one of them . . . I felt myself unpleasantly struck by an impression which seemed at first to be utterly out of harmony with the thoughts that were passing through my mind, until a moment later, with an emotion so strong that tears came to my eyes, I recognized how very much in harmony with them it was. [. . .] My first reaction had been to ask myself, angrily, who is this stranger who was coming to trouble me. The stranger was none other than myself, the child I had been at the time, brought to life within me by the book, which knowing nothing of me except this child had instantly summoned him to its presence . . . And this book which my mother had read aloud to me at Combray until the early hours of the morning . . .* The sweetness of his return recaptures the force of the innocence, seen as innocence only retroactively. This landmark by its startling appearance pronounces the unexpected arrival of the end.

The two books encircle the book and lend it closure—open it and close it as one phenomenon—exactly this way: the first book, the book of innocence, captures the image of experience; the second book, the book of experience, returns the image of innocence. By image, we mean potentiality, as the seed in the apple bears the image of the tree. By experience, we mean the embedding of image into world, a descent, and also a loss of image, or at least a confusion, or profusion, of images. This accounts for experience's delayed self-recognition. The difference of the lamp precedes the repetition of the light.

A sentence builds a bridge over time
Hawthorns repeating the sunlight as scent
Pink skin beneath freckles pink flower beneath petals
The new man in the arms of the old

*

He could not fall in love without first breathing in
The hawthorn opened an unknown door
Perception is the golden key thought turns in the lock
The blossom dropped the bridal chamber over his head

*

A bridge builds a sentence over time
The first word an article often or the subject itself
Calling the present tense out of the scented air
A bridge that ends at nothing or at another bridge

This is precisely why *the intelligence always comes after*. **There is no Logos; there are only hieroglyphs,** and to think is to interpret and to translate. *The essences are at once the thing to be translated and the translation itself, the sign and the meaning. They are involved in the sign in order to force us to think; they develop in the meaning in order to be necessarily conceived. The hieroglyph is everywhere; its double symbol is the accident of the encounter and the necessity of thought: "fortuitous and inevitable."*

What then do we mean by closure, in the statement: *the two books encircle the book and lend it closure—open it and close it as one phenomenon.* Two images of books bookend the project of the book in a double action that frames and clarifies the project as a search. The two images, one of experience anticipated by innocence, the other of innocence recollected by experience, reflect one another in countermovement. From the vantage point of one, the other moves in retrograde: west to east across the sky. These opposite movements capture, at the scale and measure of a life, the double force of the hieroglyph, the accident of the encounter and the retroactive necessity of thought. The contradiction inherent in the phrase "fortuitous and inevitable" proposes the porous totality of closure in the neurological sense: *the tendency of the brain to integrate signals with whatever interactions are available to it.* Completeness is always a process undergoing revision. At every point, the book can appear finished. Each return of an image in the project of the book re-closes that image. Closure furthermore depends on failure to notice the blind spot; anosognosia, the unawareness of the existence of illness, or of a lack, gap, or absence in the picture of reality. Thus at every moment, I confuse what I know of my life with everything there is to know of a life. The act of learning, of reinterpreting the hieroglyph, insists itself on me in the form of rupture, interruption, disequilibrium. Learning punches a hole in the fabric of reality. This is the accident of the encounter. Intelligence comes after, and reweaves a new pattern. *I saw everything reel, as one does when one falls from a horse, and I asked myself whether there was not an existence altogether different from the one I knew, in direct contradiction to it, but itself the real one, which, being suddenly revealed to me, filled me with that hesitation which sculptors, in representing the Last Judgment,*

Memory larval in mind this honey in its cell
Waking in the summer heat expanding
Ancestors buried beneath the stones she sits upon
Her lax gaze alive is the line by which the dead escape

*

The grave confines a content that leaks out
The steeples shifting relation as the carriage moves
Ahead of the dust its own wheels rise into clouds
To speak of it before night abandons us to our rooms

*

In our thoughts there is no us only this me
Seeing again that the sunlight fell on the steeple
In a perfect square memory pushes down walls
Time erects dust within a shaft of light

have given to the awakened dead who find themselves at the gates of the next world. Yet the bookends remain intact—only the distance between them elongates, and the inflection of their contents deepen and transform, for there is no intervention into my life that I cannot absorb as my life. In this sense, the essences of the events of my life *are at once the thing to be translated and the translation itself*. Time undergoes continual collapse and reconstruction. The future contains the past, and the past the future, as images nesting in experience, images that reappear under constant reconstruction. The future's arrival expresses itself in resemblance to a phrase whose music repeats, and whose repetition blossoms by accident. The image takes the form of a message sent both forward and backward in time.

Exceptio probat regulum—with an aura of exception, trauma rends chronology's weave. The traumatic by definition resists absorption, obstructs time's flow and transformation into a life. The symptomology of KC clarifies memory as a triple subject. Even the minor trauma of an act of learning differentiates memory's episodic, semantic, and procedural constituents, and reveals those parts as inherently disharmonious, their apparent singularity as ephemeral, arising out of an operative and contingent harmony, a product of closure. A major trauma—KC's accident or World War I—leaves in its wake an unbridgeable aporia, and a multiple author.

Multiplicity troubles the lifelong project of the book. Yet the singularity of subject does not melt into air, rendering the project subjectless, or even somehow focused on the absence of subject and the impossibility of experience, as has been argued: *there is no longer really any subject, but only—with singular materialism—an infinite drifting and a casual colliding of objects and sensations . . .* As the individual transforms into a succession of individuals, the subject undergoes a perpetual dance of constitution and reconstitution. Philosophically, to confuse the multiple with the nonexistent mistakes the more for the less. Neurologically, to bemoan the nuance of subject multiplicity as *absent* subject replays the error of the nonexistent executive. One mourns the loss of an illusion of one's own creation, an illusion supplied to simplify the complexity of actual brain function. A brain, constituted of independent parts,

Expectation weaves its tapestry before the day
Rends apart the seams and with its light arrives
The present tense seen through a window
Age ambers ripples so to see at all is to see as if

*

Through water a transparence that also reflects
The light on the surface that ruptures the plane
A barrier to the same world it reveals
Mind swallowing light behind the mouth in the eye

*

The day weaves desire into these hands that fail
To embrace or be embraced as a scent embraces
The air waking desire so waking death
The pollen embalmed in the page's amber elegy

synchronizes without the guidance of a single authority. We may liken the mysterious effect to an orchestra playing perfectly with no conductor. We must challenge our own differentiations between musician, bandleader, and audience, and conclude that rather than a subjectless universe, we have entered a universe of subject to the Nth degree.

A shorthand double question then describes the lifelong book project in general: what produces closure? how does the multiple cohere? The first asks about the formation of a world, the second about the formation of a life. The two questions branch from the quest that guides the project: what constitutes (and perpetually reconstitutes) individual experience? We begin to grasp time's essential role in the project when we understand how one apprehends the (literary) subject as *retrospective hypothesis*, a turn of phrase echoic of neurology's characterization of brain-based epistemology as *retrospective prophecy*. Both phrases attempt to name the same disturbance between future and past. The disturbance testifies to the success of the lifelong book project, a success that both regains and obliterates times. The question follows regarding relations between subject and object in such a universe. Does the object undergo the same dance, or a similar one, of construction and reconstruction, of capture and recapture by the subject? How can we understand the encounter between *two separate and immanent dynamisms related by no system of synchronization*? We may address the questions by revisiting *salience* in its clinical usage:

   . . . the appearance of salient houses.

One could recognize the steeple of Saint-Hilaire from quite far off inscribing its unforgettable form on the horizon where Combray had not yet appeared; when from the train which, in Easter week, was bringing us from Paris, my father caught sight of it as it slipped by turns over all the furrows of the sky and sent its little iron weathercock running in all directions, he would say to us: 'Come, gather up the rugs, we're here.'

We may note the orienting spire of the Saint-Hilaire church in Combray as the quintessential *landmark* with respect to the five guiding elements of environment imageability and wayfinding: path, edge, district, node, and landmark. How does the image of the spire stake its claims in salience, the quality of standing out relative to neighboring

I walked in my childhood certain paths and on these paths saw certain persons and things repeatedly in my own eyes.
Had I lived elsewhere I would have lived a different life. A different vision enters through the same eyes
And the impulse to speak would have emerged from my hand or mouth in a cadence differently shaped,
Obsessed with things now of no concern or interest to me; I might paint; I might compose
A sonata whose musical structure mimics the slight changes in elevation of this other path I walk on, a nameless
Suspense around the same corner, this other life I've walked countless times around, never ceasing to be surprised.

*

I put away the small fiction of my life after I had almost finished living it. Images were not the point I was after.
He let his erotic fascinations develop outside his aesthetic concerns, a man I knew as a child, and admired, a man
I almost became. A little love song, just a few notes played on the piano, skillfully or artlessly, divorced from the context
Of the musical whole, the concerto he would never hear, the little musical theme that merged in his mind
His own life with the life of the woman he loved, asking her to play it for him, intimacy wandering a path
In his ear, naming what he could find no name for: finding behind her too large eyes the master staring back out.

images? The steeple's appearance announces arrival, in both the physical landscape of Combray and the temporal landscape of the book. Its landmark function doubles as a literary marker, orienting the reader in the passage—a psychic gateway to the secondary childhood environment that Combray represents relative to Paris. It attains its landmark status in part by virtue of its being the tallest thing in this particular terrain. We may consider it similar in this respect to the Buddhas of The Silk Road, or the twin towers of the World Trade Center, two dual targets of twenty-first century iconoclasm. Allow me to persist in this digression long enough to ask: what icons were overthrown with the destruction of these landmarks? To what extent do the targets owe their salience to their character as images in sacred sign systems, versus their secular simplicity as *the tallest thing*? Boston columnist James Carroll wrote the following pertinent passage in the aftermath of the destruction of the golden dome and minarets of the Askariya mosque in Samarra.

When I was a boy living in Germany, son of a U.S. Air Force officer, nothing demonstrated the virtue·of American war making methods better than the fact that U.S. bombers had spared the magnificent Cologne cathedral, which dated to the Middle Ages and the spires of which were the tallest structures in Europe until the Eiffel Tower. Oddly, the photos that showed the wholly devastated urban core of Cologne, with the soaring church standing alone amid rubble stretching to the horizon, left me feeling proud. In my immature mind, the virtue of the American military's not having attacked that church trumped the horror of its obliteration of the whole population. I wrote of this before, and a reader, a veteran target-picker from the Eighth Air Force, snorted at the legend, telling me that the Cologne cathedral had been spared because its spires were an essential navigational aid.

The pinpoint destruction of the Buddha statues and the World Trade Center inverts the Cologne formula. Instead of obliterating an entire population around a point of orientation, the "target-pickers" obliterate the point of orientation at the heart of an entire population. The repercussive trauma, like that of KC, manifests waves of disorientation.

The hieroglyph nature of the steeple of Saint-Hilaire, its presence as a *salient house* in the memory landscape, from its first glimpse inaugurates

Memory needs no wine spilled on the ground to seduce her into clarity, nor is ink on the page
A libation. Memory carries within herself her own living waters:
A stream that dives underground when bidden by thirst, a fountain when forgotten.
My dear, my hand is shaking so hard I can scarcely write sealed in the envelope in which her shaking hand
Arrived, locked in the dark desk he avoids nearing, lest he open the drawer, and missing her,
Not knowing with whom she spends those hours she refuses him, read again her words and remember the truth

*

In which the truth begins to revel. To lie to someone is also to hope the deceit charms. Truth is a blind
Impulse to which memory adds eyes. One needs to be another self to judge with clarity the self one is.
Memory sings no aria. Memory is that chorus whose countless voices sing from within a single throat
Truth threatens to dispel the music we listen to, tied to the mast of our own life, lusting for she who sings,
The siren, from the shoals within our own ear, a voice singing in our voice, other self we must sing to remember
Us as she once saw us, this me I could be, had been, beneath the whirlpool, where the drowned men warn Fate repeats . . .

an oscillation between two opposing iconographies—the forces of sacred and secular. The father, cued by the steeple, tells the family to *gather up the rugs*. He does not tell them to pray. The steeple's salience arises primarily from its physical existence. It stands out relative to those elements around it because of its relationship to the clouds, its bridging of earth and sky. Second, the affixing to it of such concrete geographic meaning places it outside the religious sign system of its intent. The concurrence that the steeple carries meaning, but the obversion of the meaning it is meant to carry, drives a wedge between its existence as stone and symbol. This seed planted at the book's outset flowers into the hamartiology, the *missing the mark*, that the book will work out as a thorough sign system in retrograde movement relative to theology. The same church, its Chapel of Gilbert the Bad, soon houses the first sighting of the Duchesse de Guermantes, from which resemblances of Gilberte in appearance and name will telescope. Decades later a remark as offhand as the father's on the train will close the thread with the same delicacy. The father's voice has been supplanted by that of Charlus, discussing the role of the Americans in the war. *" . . . Combray was simply a small town like hundreds of others. But the ancestors of my family were portrayed as donors in some of the windows in the church, and in others our armorial bearings were depicted. And now this church has been destroyed by the French and the English because it served as an observation-post to the Germans."* The narrator seems hardly to register the destruction, perhaps because by then he has established the indelibility of the Church of Saint-Hilaire in his heart. He corrects the Baron. *"You mean its symbol, Monsieur," I interrupted. "And I adore certain symbols no less than you do. But it would be absurd to sacrifice to the symbol the reality that it symbolizes. Cathedrals are to be adored until the day when, to preserve them, it would be necessary to deny the truths which they teach. The raised arm of St Firmin said, with an almost military gesture of command: 'Let us be broken if honour requires.' Do not sacrifice men to stones whose beauty comes precisely from their having for a moment given fixed form to human truths."*

The hamartiological strategy does not aspire to destroy the image; it depends on the image, both physical and symbolic, for its existence. It

. . . in the mind, the heavier ocean whose waves break darkly upon the day, stranding the margins in wakefulness,
Another drowned man whose face, turned upward in the light, is our own. Growing lack of a single self
Is my own wit a return, beneath the chandeliers, to that man I am, at the princess's elbow, the gossip in the party
A cloud within the music's larger sphere, speaking as a violin speaks clearly against the notes, betraying
With its own melody the swelling music beneath it that birthed it, making of music a silence on which its own desire,
Almost human, almost more than human, in its urgency, is written, before descending again into the noise

*

And by its descent, transforming the noise back into symphony, these notes any violin can play, the song singing out
The hollow body, this music anyone can own, this voice anyone can speak, anyone can make one's own, this beauty
That strikes at the heart as if to stop it, that hollow chamber always filling with blood, that blood that belongs
To everyone, resonating to a pulse it produces but cannot play, a rhythm one must steady one's hand against, to calm
Oneself, to seem calm to another, to appear self-possessed, recovered, unharmed by the rumors everyone repeats,
To speak intelligently, that language for which I'm known, when I am me, that saying one thing, always means another.

proliferates counter-meanings, attaching as a parasite to a host. For the father on the train, the steeple's landmark quality constitutes its *only* spiritual symbolism. As the father defines the world, as a surrogate *God the Father*, the failure of his patronage to note the steeple as church, his recognition of it only as *the tallest thing*, constitutes the hamartia, the generative error in judgment arising from ignorance or moral shortcoming, which initiates a tragic journey. The father's blindspot produces the philosophy of the son. Hamartia becomes hamartiology, obvert engenders invert, and the method developed over the years of the book for navigation according to the salient houses of time's landscapes becomes an inverse theology, and a tragic miracle.

While time perpetually revises both object and subject, within the confines of the project, object remains stable relative to subject—narrator changes more rapidly and radically than steeple. The individual coheres as a succession of individuals, apprehended in retrospect; the steeple remains exempt from that intrinsic flux. We may consider the subject's succession of selves the product of the ongoing practices of rupture and restabilization produced by the oscillations between habit and memory. As experience becomes memory and memory habit, a new *learning* episode forces a change in sign signification, which must rupture habit in order to become a new lasting memory, and eventually a new habit. Now we may multiply this procedure by three, as we consider memory triple. Semantic memory constantly revises names and their attachment to signifiers. Procedural memory reinscribes behavior, and how the self acts and perfects actions. Episodic memory revisits events in sequence, and the place of the self in them. The three distinct consistencies of the three forms of memory rupture and restore themselves differently. Does the young woman glimpsed behind the hawthorn hedge fit in the container of the same name as the young woman whose features echo in the window of the Chapel of Gilbert the Bad? Does one remove one's boots the same way in the low-ceilinged bedroom at home as in the high-ceilinged room at the inn? How does the landscape in which two walks nearly intersect coincide with the two landscapes of the same two walks, remote and separate? In each case, the subject, the self-image,

The eye accustoms itself to details, a vision in infinite regress, a scrutiny learned to detach the self that suffers
Enchantment from the object, as light from a single source appears on every surface of the crystal
Chandelier, as that unlidded crystal, the human eye, is a surface the jeweler makes so multi-faceted it appears round
As the light falling into it also dances on its surface, the dark lashes coyly obscuring the light, as a lover,
In the carriage at night, might put her hand before the moon and mask its light with her fingers
Only to turn the moon more brilliant by placing her hand suddenly on my heart, where earlier she looked at me

*

As she looks at no one else—she who enchants. A detail is a certain kind of faith—almost a philosophy, almost a logic—
That believes appearance hides a fact, and to discover the fact, dispels the appearance. Beauty and Truth laugh
When they hold hands, walking through the *tromp l'oeil* garden, the nymphs with their hands open beneath the lamps,
The forest stream that ends in the champagne flute, where the musicians play, and in the ear of this one I am, in my ear,
I know there is another room, a room with no doors, in which she whom I love and another sit, a flute
Flitting a tune through the leaves painted on one wall, as if there were no wall, fooling the eye that wants to be fooled.

and not the object, undergoes radical, even catastrophic, revision; the narrator in perceiving a difference in the object does not perceive the object as changed, but only his previous perception as having been imperfect. What he accepted as whole has been recast as provisional. The narrator must then rewrite not only his present, but also his entire past with its flawed foundation. Thus the self, made of memory, replaces itself, and renews itself, with each successive revelation. The action of the book unfolds within the body of the narrator. For the scrub jay, the pine nut remains a pine nut for as long as necessary. In recovering it unchanged, the scrub jay encounters itself as the youthful scrub jay who once, so long ago, buried the pine nut in precisely that place. The grub however stays a grub for only five days. Yet time does not destroy the grub, but only transforms it into the not-grub, something inedible. The destruction of the steeple of Saint-Hilaire at Combray cannot be iconoclastic, since the icon, the image, resides only partly in the physical carrier. For the narrator the cathedral gives a *human truth* form on the landscape of the heart, a temporal sight on memory's train journey. The outpost for the Germans that has been destroyed had never been written into the object. The finger in the sky, the name, the navigation point in the landscape, the landmark in time, endures.

The ordinary definitions of *book* as a form of recording accounts— of financial records, of guests visiting a house—underpin my usage of the word in the phrase *the book at the end of the book.* If *Francois de Champi* by George Sand landmarks the terminal moment of the quest, recapitulating the *miracle of the courtyard* with its uneven paving stone, it does so doubly—once as an image recurring from childhood, and again because of the accidental work the image does of accounting the narrator's life. I use the word *account* in relation to *witness*: one who is answerable for, or literally who counts, in this case the years between the object's first and final appearances in the life, and does so by virtue of the stable position of such an object—book, steeple—relative to the verisimilitudes and revisions of the life. The stability of the book witnesses, testifies to, even accounts for, how much we have changed since last we saw it. We measure our change against its sameness, variants

Desire finds within a surface a depth it wants to enter. Erotic madness sees in the surface of her eyes
A depth that swallows whole we who look into her eyes. In moments of sexual bliss she closes her eyes
And then we are cut off from the sun, cut off from the moon and the stars, cut off from Venus's little pin
Beneath the shallow bowl of moon, then darkness undoes us, all of us, all of us who gather together
In my name, who remember certain moments that repeat in the mind, prefaced by music we could not hear
While we were alive, unsung melodies of the spheres, wandering the streets at night to that music, memory

*

Orchestrating the mind, these repeated themes, the cafes she might have dined in, the candle-lit rooms
Where she laughed, might have laughed, might have opened her closed lids into slits her dark eyes
Rolling down to the corner, a little seeing-jewel on her ear, a little ornament coming unpinned from her lobe . . .
We've seen it. We've seen it as we wandered the streets calling out her name, each one of us
I am when I am all of us, standing below the lit window, imagining her in another man's embrace in that light,
Knocking our hand against it, that window not hers . . . Our mistake was a question we were asking about time.

against its ostinato. Let us place *Francois de Champi* by George Sand beside the book that the narrator dreams at the outset, and ask how these two books speak to one another, and what relation they may share to the goal. The dream immerses the narrator in the completed book of experience, in the dream that escapes telos by existing like music already wholly within it. The dreamed book merges the self who lives with the self who writes, as a weave of the major motifs of the temporal landscapes—a church, a war, a sonata. The dreamed book proposes the possibility of accounting. It allows and instigates the labor of the life by virtue of the life being already complete at any moment. The dreamed book is the book of closure. It is the goal the traveler carries within him as he pursues the goal—the goal in the heart defining the goal in the world. It is the book inside the book, and the book that the book is inside. *Francois de Champi* by George Sand differentiates itself from the dreamed book to the extent that a beginning and an ending are separate from one another. Are they? We find a beginning at every beginning, as we find an end at every end. We may consider them nonidentical twins; with the arising of each there will also arise the other. What then do I mean by *end*? Consider the word *bookend* as both noun and verb. If one lacks a proper bookend on an open bookshelf, one might use the largest available book turned on its side. The book then bookends. It remains itself, but by virtue of its bigness it holds the other books in place. One may think of the first *book* in my title as the shelf. This is the life project of the book. It overflows its frame or any frame because its bigness forestalls any approach to singularity. We can by no means accurately consider it one book, one project, any more than we can consider a city one building. It is an aggregate—a multiplicity that coheres under a single name, and its fundamental strategy of closure is the double bookend. Without them, the project remains many books on a shelf. With them, it coheres into many books becoming one. So we might say the bookends at the end of the book are the largest books possible, the landmarks, deployed to hold the project in place at its end, while the project is the one book that exceeds the biggest possible book by being many books, made into one by their presence and in relation to their ends.

When do we accept who we are? I like to think about myself as a child when I liked to think about myself
As a grown man, rare in taste, endlessly writing a short essay on Vermeer, asking the Prince to create a diversion
While I plunged the flower on its stem deeper into the maid's décolletage. When do I accept that this me is me?
Sometimes I think about myself as a child thinking about myself as a grown man thinking about others
He thinks he might also be. How could I know time was passing while I thought these thoughts?
As a child I often wondered what it would mean to be somebody, somebody who had a life, somebody who

*

In that life thought about who he was, and what it meant to be who he was. When do you accept
The evidence that this you is who you are? When do you? If it seems I am talking to myself
It is because I am so tired of talking to no one. I don't mean to deny your hand that may be reading
This page even as I write it. I don't mean to deny you may be holding me. I don't mean to deny
You might be thinking these thoughts for me, now that I am dead, if I am dead. When do we accept
That the little iron weathercock running in all directions on the steeple-top is a figure of us all—

I intend the word *end* not only as *the outside or extreme edge or limit of something, the boundary*, but also as *the point in time at which an action, event, or phenomenon ceases or is completed, the conclusion*, and even as *a goal toward which one strives*. The books at the end of the book fulfill each of these dictionary definitions simultaneously. I have said enough about the first two. I will conclude by lingering for a moment on the third, the goal of the book project of a life. The book concludes with the definitive discovery that the goal of transtemporality, of the obliteration (regaining) of time through resurgent involuntary memory asserts itself as a phenomenon only by accident. The primary force of the accidental in regaining time conforms to three patterns. Accident #1: chronology—event *b* follows event *a* for no apparent reason. Accident #2: coincidence—event *a'* occurs simultaneously with event *a*, also for no apparent reason. Accident #3: echo—event *aa* resembles event *a*, or appears to, because of the singular perceptual faculties of the observer. The Easter Week appearance of the steeple in motion, followed by the father's words, followed by the appearance of Combray takes accident form #1. Madeleine and lime infusion coinciding with rainy Combray takes accident form #2. Once again KC's damage throws into stark relief the dependence of functional memory on these three forms of accident. Given the discovery of memory's structures and constraints, does the goal become a double weave, dependent primarily on accident for its occurrence, and secondarily on persistent will for the retroactive inscription of meaning?

In the braid of these two strands, a third end takes shape, as the alignment of the will of the narrator and the will of the unknown (the accident) engenders a secular religion. The ultimate revelation, for which the George Sand book serves as a capstone, resembles nothing more than epiphany, *the miracle of the courtyard*; that the resurgence of overlooked similarity, no matter how ordinary, produces a life worth living, as the self and the memory of the self, the will and the accident, meet in an undifferentiated life force. I am the accident of my memory. Memory then takes the form of a minor trauma, a jolt to itself, as the scrub jay knows where the pine nut lies, but not exactly what the pine nut is,

Wonder closes
Desire defies
Eyes to open
    other eyes
    light enters with
    a vision
The eye emits

*

When she spoke
    over her shoulder
    my name
I felt I was
    in the park in
    winter
Alive
And naked
    in her mouth

until the shock of re-encounter, and the folding back of time upon itself. Memory's miracle, its inverse religion, its merging of self and nonself, completes, *ends* one might say, the quest of, and for, experience. It does so within the frame and form of the book.

Eros in the ground dusk divides
Night from day
    Earth from sky
Eros hidden in the games

Children play a love that learns

To act a hatred that costumes heaven

*

I knew I was old
    when in the woods
    the nymphs
    walked under winter
Memory a bridal veil
    defining
    hem-loose threads
The bare branch a flowering
    arbor
    arching over the distant
Nuptial leaf-hidden lake's
    ice
Ice

PART 2:
THE LONG SENTENCE

is serpentine, and like a snake, moves forward by first constricting itself
into clauses which, like the teeth of an ancient snake sown into the ground,
threaten to become another life, a life that rises up from the blank
field armed, belligerent, that kills the brothers birthed from the same mouth,
the mouth of the mother, and those lives that remain alive build the walls
of the city they live within, raising families, adding flesh to bone,
living children whose fathers are made of stone   the long sentence is

a wall more solid for being always broken, a barrier that cannot be scaled,
no segment remaining static, each stone containing within it
a little room in which the household gods live, an empty space,
an altar an image fills when the word is read, when the reader, barbarian,
knocks against the wall by reading it with an axe or a flame in his mind

heir only honor is precarious, their only liberty provisional until the crime be discovered . . .

So begins the 953-word sentence that marks the project's midpoint. As I read my way through the seven novels, I sensed their background architectural structure unfolding. The temporal shifts at discontinuous breaks between chapters, parts, or books, versus the continuous threads of extended passages, the recurring evolving motifs, seemed conceived with vast rhythms in mind, like the immense massings and fine details of a cathedral. The project at times announces that intention. But the long sentence, while not entirely unexpected, since I anticipated a gesture of halfway there where the smallish section that starts the fourth book falls, arrested me nevertheless with its relentless extremity. One can only attempt a structural reading in earnest retrospectively, after having finished the project and looking back. As a child alone on the playground, I walked the teeter-totter from one end to the other, enjoying the liftoff, balance, and suspension before incline becomes decline, but always landed with a crash no matter how I shifted my weight to control the plank. The long sentence struck me as that fulcrum moment, a catastrophe of event and mathematics. When one senses that a journey's midpoint has been reached, does the realization always manifest as disorientation *in a dark wood wandering?* Do such points of equivalence between past and future demand reversal and redirection? In this case, what exactly tips? A restricted set of concepts has been introduced: transtemporality asserts itself through signifiers; memory's force overflows into present fact, with accompanying accidental proximal sensations, capable of transporting the subject's consciousness across time. But now a rupture occurs. In this project that has meticulously elaborated its foundation on deciphering *the mystery of the other* entirely and discretely as a formation of observable exterior signs, the revelation of the lie carries violent implications. Now images exist not only to misdirect, but also to communicate secrets to those with the encryption's key. Signifier and reader divide, and the moment halves the project in its relation to image—its first built of innocence; its second of tragic experience—the two bridged by the span of the long sentence.

. . . their love . . . springs not from an ideal of beauty which they have chosen but from an incurable disease . . .

Before it begins there is a man telling us he is dying, a man mired
in a shameful marriage (all this is descriptive) his friends choose to ignore,
a man who says he is dying as the duchesse returns to her bedroom
to find her red shoes, she had mistakenly worn her black shoes,
the red shoes are for the party, the black shoes are for home or for death.
After the long sentence the dying man arrives
at the party where the duchesse wears her red shoes and does not see him
or seeing him from the corner of her eyes pretends not to see him.
There is a rumor after the long sentence that the dying man has been denied.
On either end of the long sentence the same man is dying.
He is dying in a different way each time.
Inside the long sentence we sense there is an exclusive form of life
and those of us dying want to be let in, and when we are let in
we are still dying, but no one will admit it, no one will state the fact
that the eye has no corners. To say the eye has a corner is to lie.

A brain infection (herpes encephalitis) struck the eminent English musician, permanently inflicting him with the most debilitating amnesia ever documented. The account kept by his wife records an incident, early in the illness, in which she discovers him *holding something in the palm of one hand, and repeatedly covering and uncovering it with the other hand as if he were a magician practicing a disappearing trick. He was holding a chocolate. He could feel the chocolate unmoving in his left palm, and yet every time he lifted his hand he told me it revealed a brand new chocolate.*

"Look!" he said. "It's new!" *He couldn't take his eyes off it.* "It's the same chocolate," *I said gently.* "No . . . look! It's changed. It wasn't like that before . . ."

The entries of the journal he began at this time consisted of the statements *I am awake* or *I am conscious* entered repeatedly: *2.10 pm: this time properly awake . . . 2.14 pm: this time finally awake . . . 2.35 pm: this time completely awake,* along with their negations: *At 9.40 pm I awoke for the first time, despite my previous claims.*

Over the years he managed a degree of ordinary existence. He demonstrated an almost compulsive loquacity in order to function, as if without conversation the void could engulf him. Separated briefly from his wife in the supermarket, he suddenly exclaimed *I'm conscious now . . . never saw a human being before . . . for thirty years . . . It's like death!* In such circumstances he lapsed into sustained speech of anger and distress, expressing absolute existence in the present moment, the remembered now, fully awake always for the first time. The staff of the facility in which he lived referred to these monologues as his *deads.*

How then, in this condition, was he able to sit at the piano and flawlessly play Bach's *Prelude 9 in E major?*

Because its length moves it creates motion and so creates time.
It becomes mortal in the same instant it becomes alive.
A darker sentence occurs simultaneously beneath the sentence
whose language we know and read, a language of shades
beneath a language of sense, a form of fate, unutterable
translation of sound into shadow, writhing beneath the world—

world

the long sentence wants never to end.

While he could not remember that he could play, with a score before him, he executed his musical abilities as precisely as he had before the amnesia. Can his playing, his singing, his conducting, his powers of improvisation, be adequately characterized as *skills* or *procedure*? Can *procedural memory* describe any creative performance of this caliber? *Episodic memory* depends on the perception of particular events, in the form of memories not only highly individual (inflected by interests, concerns and values), but prone to revision at each recollection. This contrasts fundamentally with the literalness, exactitude, and reproducibility of *procedural memory*. Perhaps a nuanced area of intersection exists, a meeting place of these two forms of memory, in the *fixed action pattern*, the activity both created and repeated at once, present at birth, yet learned through a lifetime. The fetal horse gallops in the womb. The adult horse gallops in tune with the ground. The musician's wife speaks of observing the importance of the *momentum* of music. Every bar, every phrase, arises from what preceded and decays into what follows through built-in dynamism. It may be that the musician, incapable of remembering or anticipating events because of his amnesia, can sing and play and conduct because remembering music does not, in the usual sense, involve remembering at all. Remembering, listening to, or playing music transpires entirely in the present. The melody, like the sentence, unwinds *one thought from beginning to end*.

It creates a wound underneath itself it cannot heal.
All that limits us it seems to penetrate; it seems to find within us
a wound that does not heal. It gives us certain signs
so we remember to breathe, but it lives without breath.
When it breathes it borrows from us a quality
it otherwise cannot possess. An open mouth
expresses anger or desire, sorrow or surprise, shortness of breath.
A kind of wound in our face that exposes us to others—
a nakedness one cannot hide, but tries to mask
with words, as if my mouth were open to speak about the flowers
in this late season just now in bloom, or about the clouds,
or in denying I feel pain that I am hearing the piano being tuned
in the other room: "No, I'm fine, I'm fine. Do you hear the music?
Do you know the tune?" But I wanted to kiss you. A kind of pain.
I was possessed of wanting to kiss you. My mouth was open
when the long sentence ended. Needing breath; it inflicted desire.

Kairos, the Greek concept of the perishable duration of the opportunity—*it is the time, it is the moment*—connotes the time of circumstance, *heterogeneous*, different from other times. Recognizing the *Kairos* demands the neutral attention to the singular character of the now. Skilled speakers among the Sophists claimed to possess total knowledge and the ability to address any subject, their orations seizing the words called for by the moment. They founded extemporaneous speaking, the art of the opportune instant, described as *kairou chronou techne*— the creative technique of weaving the time of the clock with the time of the event. The discipline practiced a quality of attention, intuitive and perhaps systematic. We might consider *kairou chronou techne* the practice of *unfixing* the fixed action pattern, attuned to the moment of the pattern's disturbance, that demands a revision and redirection, the capture of the force of the rupture.

The narrator did not want to risk being seen by those he watched,
those two men in the courtyard nearing one another and entering
the tailor's shop, so the narrator kept himself hidden as he walked.
There are many ways the narrator knows to remain invisible
to those he watches: passageways in which the slats of the drawn blinds
let through enough light to see the stairs. Dust is here
in this thought, in this thinking, and in dust traces are left of a
presence which did not linger. Sometimes the speaker stays silent
and hidden within his own face, a passage we call memory
or mind, an eye that watches behind the eye, containing its own vision,
in a face beneath the face, turned inward, looking at itself looking—
as the doctor notices two girls dancing and points out desire
flushing their cheeks red as their breasts touch—at a photograph
taken by the sea, black hat covering the downward slope of her mouth
after the stroke, the dust on the glass, the photo of grandmother,
of she who has died, suddenly remembered in the mind and alive
inside the dust, within the dust, leaving her thumbprint on the glass.
The narrator does not want to risk being seen behind his mask.
Others talk to us but our minds may be elsewhere. We talk to them
to distract them, to hope they do not see we are not there with them.
The long sentence distracts them while we rummage through the box.
One image sees ourselves with our hands inside our heads.
Another image sees the Baron's cock in the tailor's mouth.
Memory and desire: dimly lit stairs within the stare. They have a face.

The perishable moment intervenes into the cathedral form of the project. How does the rupture situate within, or, at its appearance, as a point outside of, that elaborate construction? In the narrative, a moment arrives and the narrator recognizes and seizes its opportunity, as he has come to value the unsettled feeling it precipitates in him, his perception, his sensation; the recognition, the misrecognition. This moment in question, and the moment and method of its seizing, become the centerpoint of the project. The catastrophe is the overturning of image itself: the notion heretofore examined so intensively as to become the project's foundation, that images record the truth; they encode in their sensations a reclaimable past. Now that foundation abruptly suffers a seismic rift, and out of the rift the becoming emerges—the dual mistaken identity of the wasp that sees in the orchid another wasp. The orchid's mimicry induces the collapse, because a flower's appearance provokes the memory of an insect. The retraced lineage of all such flowering deceivers delivers a deeper and more nuanced definition of image, as the simultaneous potentiality of echo and mimic. The project's developing hamartiology takes a monumental step at the moment of this telescoping revelation: image contains deception contains violence. *The movement by which reality exceeds its definition* goes retrograde in the long sentence's naming of the inverts.

The desire to think complicates the music
that myth about the world that it exists
in the long sentence there is that rumor we rely on
that we exist in the long sentence and the
world exists. I could try to describe the music
but would only describe myself or a process
that occurring in me seems like myself
the long sentence of being someone like myself
who exists. This music desires thought
disguises melody with words
the long sentence speaks over the music
it contains and hides the music in speaking
the men and women who in the sentence live
act as if they are not dancing; they do not know
they are dancing; they speak but do not
know in their speech they are singing;
they do not hear the tune composing them.
Fate is one form the long sentence may take
and one might ask, each one of us might ask,
where does fate end and this is a question
the long sentence answers by ending.

Biographers have characterized his writing rituals as precisely this: life lived up to a point of rupture, followed by a period of retreat, withdrawing into silence, and then a clinical observation and retracing of the steps leading up to and including the catastrophe; that is, catastrophic in its reframing the past irrevocably as past. This overly simple formula does not do justice to the complexity of the practice, yet the architecture of collapse may guide our reading. The death of the mother precipitates the sanitarium stay and ultimately the birth of the project. The seven novels replay this scheme, this theme, in major and minor keys, repeatedly and in infinite variation.

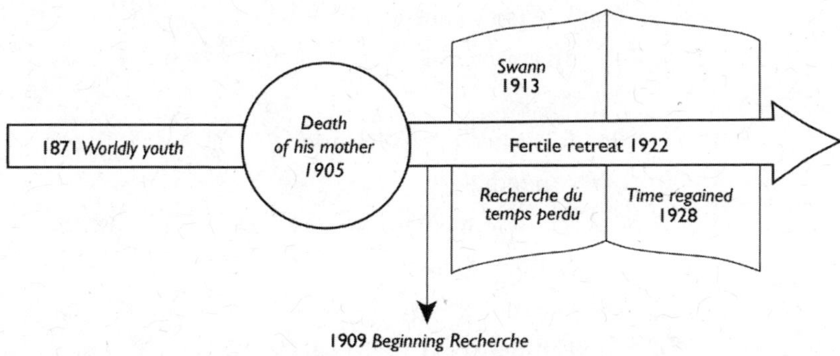

Regarding syntax, then, what role does the sentence play in the project, and why must the narrator render the revelation of the Baron and the tailor as the longest of sentences?

THE LONG SENTENCE (11)

a pillow, a mirror
an ideal beauty
  seeking out
desire

ecstasy also strikes
  Socrates
    (so peculiar
an example)

faith better understood
  needs
knowledge (the
beggar-secret)

the wildly private part
  suspected
    it does not
exist

found out about language that paragraphs are emotional and sentences are not and I found out something else about it. I found out that this difference was not a contradiction but a combination and that this combination causes one to think endlessly about sentences and paragraphs because the emotional paragraphs are made up of unemotional sentences.

The sentence in question embeds itself in a paragraph bracketed by several sentences before it and only one after it. Before the long sentence: *I understood . . . !* the force of the rupture captured, then rendered as indicator of "race." After the long sentence, the paragraph simply states, as if having proven a theorem, the existence of two radically opposed societies, one telescoped within the other precisely as the Baron's image doubles and telescopes into itself; a failed assimilation, an uneasy *passing as* other. The emotion, one might say, arises from the combined syntactic journey, the time that passes in the paragraph, the difference between the world at its start and the world at its end. Yet the long sentence undergoes its own journey. It is a sentence becoming paragraph perhaps, by virtue of its extreme elongation and elasticity, its tumbling down the slope to keep pace with, or regain the balance of the project after, the catastrophic drop of the rupture. This regaining not of time but of equilibrium requires an act of unfixing and reinscribing a *fixed action pattern*. The sentence becomes an exercise, an event of learning through an effort of its own singular duration and rhythm—self-characterized early on as that of *turning the millstone like Samson.*

Why must this event proceed without interruption, as a single sentence? Certainly to some degree interruption provides both its subject and catalyst. *Kairos* takes the form of the mental catastrophe that occurs in a single blow. But what is the function of non-interruption?

the poet excluded by all poetry
lips ritual desire
the physical opposing appearance
(the fact alone is more extensive)

men intend a secret in this life

but a private part does not exist

existence is its never guessed at intimacy
speaking of others
of their vocabulary which imposes upon them
themselves in such a way
that themselves do not appear

The thread of discourse—*sutra*—weaves its strand, the textile of the text. Its reverse motion unravels like the deliberate review, the ritualizing, of an initially random path, where random means following the unpredictable impulses of the investigation. The journey into the labyrinth pursues the monster through its sounds, smells, signifiers. The journey out repeats those steps in mirror reversal in time and space—two trajectories, intimate and unjoinable. Ariadne's clew does not compose the investigation, but rewinds it, and in this way through repeatability fixes it into pattern. Improvisation becomes composition. Steps become score. The ball of string must be continuous and unbroken if it is to guide its perfect escape. From the path retracing the events of the apprenticeship, the concealed music appears.

love contrived to add to love
beauty chosen from desire

but finding the least scruple
disgrace alone remained innate

*

it is shutting, the secret other
the trembling part of

the whole living intimacy
improperly called a vice

Appearing in the form of music, the thread, the melodic path of the sonata, fixes its action pattern in brain after brain across generations. Its navigation repeats and differentiates itself at each iteration. It is created and repeated at once. Remembering music does not involve memory as one normally understands memory; as such music proceeds inside of and outside of time, weaves the kairos and chronos in its (music's) technology. The action of unfixing and reinscribing the pattern must proceed without interruption, as interruption, discontinuity, assert the logic of the system, or chronos, over the logic of the event, of the kairos.

The death of the mother, the jolt of the madeleine, so many other cases, and now the incomprehensible oscillation between the Baron's two appearances—the rupture fuels the engine of the project. In retreat into a silent laboratory the writer reweaves the circumstances of the catastrophe, revealing the picture of a world of ever increasing complexity. The silence unbroken, shut off from unwanted stimuli, establishes its own circadian rhythms of work in the nycthemeron: the 24-hour cycle of day and night distinct and misaligned from the actual day and night outside. These hours of the personal day shield the mind according to the demands of its own continuity. As the afternoon sun declines unseen, the writer stirs in his bed, pulls the bell cord. Within minutes his servant companion delivers *the silver coffeepot with his initials; the lidded porcelain jug to keep the boiled milk hot; the big gold-rimmed bowl with the family monogram; the croissant, in its own saucer, from the baker in rue de la Pépinière, opposite rue d'Anjou*. The miracle of her labor and intuition makes the space for his labor. Together they have re-fixed the day to the inward demands of the work that eradicates the interruption in order to paint its portrait.

vice called the inward vocabulary
to fasten its eyes on living people

part private, part action, life in this
beggar-sign rests on cruelty

*

taking pleasure in themselves
a view concealing the fact

brought into desire: incurable
malady, ideal beauty, a word

they have been calling love

The double image of the Baron emits, disgorges, radiates, the 953-word portrait in lineage, a catechism of sorts, relearning *the very structure of appearances which are both what they are and the infinity of what they exclude*, the extended moment of the project turning its own corner, the cathedral's heart, a labyrinth in miniature, the walking of which will fix in the brain a pattern of action both inside and outside of memory, a melodic line beyond the constraints of procedure or recognition, repeated and discovered with each iteration, that *images reveal and conceal in equal measure*, thus *in this fabulous, anachronistic life, the ambassador is friends with the convict.*

sympathy at times inspires
disgust portrayed in a mirror

the only ritual
shunning desire

physical, hideous relief
injuring virtue by exalted vices

vices intend to indicate his hand
which means lack of the

human whole
everywhere among the people

they would turn away
from those they slight

so the inward does not appear

The last sentence of the previous paragraph announces the impending event. It leaves no doubt as to the reason for the methods of arrangement and the sinuous gesture of continuity, out of which an indelible comprehension will appear, recasting the interior landscape outside of memory's limits as such patterns are. It sets the stage for the long sentence's performance:

Now that the abstraction had been materialized, this creature, understood at last, had at once lost its capacity to remain invisible, and the transmutation of M. de Charlus into a new person was so complete that not only the contrasts in his face and his voice but, in retrospect, even the ups and downs in his relationship with me, all that thus far had appeared incoherent to my mind, became intelligible, showed itself to be self-evident, just as a sentence that had presented no meaning for as long as it remained broken up into letters arranged at random, expresses, if the characters find themselves restored to their rightful order, a thought we will not again be able to forget.

mirror, malady
    brought into appearance
      their own life
they unmask:

pleasure without reflecting
  disgrace
    that peculiar
faith-healing:

secret, certain, private,
  unpunished
    intimacy
with the other it of others

of things of words
  they inward called
    others
themselves

Can we name this method of *restoring to their rightful order* in one unbroken sequence the misaligned letters, characters, and notes; the conviction of the long sentence to bringing into fixed appearance the logic of the previously incomprehensible? Maybe an appropriate archaism will serve: *melopoeia*—to fashion in the form of melody.

PART 3:
WORK FROM MEMORY

One discovery I have made relatively late in life—six decades in— has been the unexpected gratification I take in the sleep of others. My own sleep has most often been the cause for some anxiety. Certainly drifting into an afternoon nap might allow for some vague, almost drunken pleasure and relief, but in the early minutes of the night I sometimes feel panicked at the onset of eight hours of blankness—of travel to a specific territory that I can count on to evaporate entirely with the sunrise, leaving no evidence of any sort other than the scrap of dream fabric, which feels less of the texture of sleep than of waking thoughts and images confused. Sleep itself, its vast neutral expanse, vanishes with waking. Perhaps sleep is nothing more than that—the act of vanishing. Many times when interrupted at sleep's threshold I am left with the sensation of tremendous speed, as if my mind and even body were suddenly capable of fleeing in some direction beyond the pull of gravity or even time. How strange to try to speak of sleep from the inside. Stranger still to realize after all these years—while carrying these fears of sleep that formed early in life—that the sleep of others can bring such reassurance. I have never had children, or I may have realized this sooner. I have seen friends who are parents take pleasure in the sleep of their babies, and not only because it affords some restful time for themselves. When holding a child in my arms, as I have done occasionally, until that child falls asleep, I have the feeling I have somehow, through a blend of calculation and intuition, created the correct circumstances, as if stage-managing the performance of the sleep of the other—the proper sounds at the perfect pitch and volume, softness of fabric, temperature, dimness, even odors. All the senses require some degree of attention. In those moments then when the breathing begins to lengthen, I have a feeling of the body achieving a simple restoration or perhaps healing, which coincides somehow with travel to places beyond my waking reach. I have facilitated that travel in a way, and perhaps this proves that fears of sleep, like mine, can be best allayed not by oneself but by another. A grown-up murmurs a lullaby. A spouse occupying half of the bed, a patient resting fitfully in a hospital, a parent worn out from a day of ordinary activity—each holds a similar charge for the wakeful overseer, as if in the understanding of the toll of a violent world and a helpless individual within it, trying to get some rest. Even in the classroom where I have been fortunate enough to spend much of my adult life, I distinctly remember in one of my first afternoon classes, while in the midst of some lecture point of great excitement to me at least, noticing one of my students beginning to nod off, and, to the astonishment of the other students and even to myself, instinctively lowering my voice. Well, I whispered, he obviously needs his rest. Who can learn anything when exhausted? The disciple Ananda stands guardian-like beside the sleeping Buddha, that nothing may disturb his entrance to Nirvana. Now on the eve of my turning sixty . . . *old clothes upon old sticks to scare a bird* . . . I wonder what my age has to do with these thoughts.

Jacqueline Risset includes a chapter titled *Sleep and the Sea* in her miniature prose encyclopedia *Sleep's Powers*. In it she invokes Thalassa, the primordial Greek sea goddess, and personification of the Mediterranean. *Each night, while asleep, the beings she bore return to her waters—to their place of origin, more distant and profound than the earth.* These offspring of Thalassa, the Telchines, had flippers for hands and the heads of dogs. Nocturnal sea creatures, by day on the island of Rhodes they invented the *useful arts,* metallurgy, and fashioning images of the gods. Risset arrives at Thalassa and her fish children by way of a citation of the Hungarian psychoanalyst Sándor Ferenczi: "Sleep, like the sea, alludes to a very ancient human state, 'Thalassa'—our aquatic ancestors." Ferenczi had completed his *Thalassa—A Theory of Genitality* in 1919, but in his 1923 introduction to the volume he offered some guarded qualifications.

> *In my speculations on the problems of genitality I boldly transferred to animals,*
> *to their organs and the parts thereof, and to their tissues, all kinds of processes*
> *with which I had become acquainted through psychoanalysis; and if with the*
> *aid of this transposition I arrived at new points of view, I nevertheless became*
> *guilty of a psychomorphism which, as a methodological excess, weighed upon*
> *my scientific conscience. On the other hand, this train of thought compelled me*

to make use of observations on animals, data from embryology, etc., as aids in the explanation of mental states; as for example the status of the psyche during coitus, in sleep, and so forth. According to my conviction at that time this too was forbidden; indeed, I had learned in school to consider it a fundamental principle of scientific work to keep strictly separated from each other the respective points of view of the natural sciences and of the mental sciences. The fact that in my speculations this rule was more honored in the breach than the observance was one of the reasons which restrained me from publishing my theory of genitality.

Ferenczi's paragraph does not rise to the level of the palinode, the song of reversal of a previously held belief, but its tone of measured remorse for the *psychomorphism* of his youth, the granting of external form in nature to the human soul, haunts its imagery of the sea at night, as if having awakened from the dream of the writing.

The sea has never played much of a part in my life, although I remember a time when Lake Michigan did. First time visitors to Chicago comment on its vastness, the perfectly level blue horizon line it draws, more sea than lake, but it seems to me the waves have an entirely different character. I have a friend who lives not far from the eastern shore on the Michigan side, who often reports on the roar of the surf at night when the wind is right, especially in late fall when trees have shed their leaves but the snow has not yet come, and sound begins to travel differently through the austere woods. I grew up on that side. My mother once snapped a photograph of my father, my brother and me all trying to leap over a wave as it rolled in at the foot of the Sleeping Bear Dunes. I must have been about five years old. We traveled there in summers and hiked across the dunes to where they gradually flattened amid windblown tufts of beachgrass into the lake. We played the impossible game of wave leaping. July waves of cerulean water rolled in wide and widely spaced. Eventually we hiked back and began the long drive home. Some forty years later, my brother attempted to re-stage the photo with himself and his daughter leaping the wave, and his wife taking the photograph. He even used black and white film, and tried to reproduce the camera angle.

The role that interests me now is that of the invisible mother, the eye behind the camera. We slept soundly in the car on the way home. These activities strike me as distinctly lake-side rather than ocean-side, and I wonder what those differences of experience might provoke in thought or writing. Now, living as I do on Lake Michigan's western shore, I think of the water as a constant background presence, its surf drowned or mocked by the city's incessant traffic. Still, over its plane—calm and smoldering in October, or overtaken by fractured ice in January—the sun rises every morning.

Twelve years ago, when I was forty-eight, I worked diligently for a short, concentrated time, on a project of collaborative writing with a very distinguished poet friend. We initiated the project on the eve of his departure from Chicago, where we were colleagues, to his new home in Colorado. We thought the project would keep us in touch, and it did for a while. We shared at that time a mutual fascination with the writing of Marcel Proust, and we had the thought to compose a volume that alternated between poetry and prose in response to the search for lost time. The poetry certainly made sense to me, and his inventive strategies endlessly absorbed and inspired me. But at a certain point, my own shortcomings began to inhibit me. I was teaching at Stanford when I had time to work on it, and on my first visit to the Green Library, the librarian told me the combined Stanford libraries held roughly six million books. I remember replying that, thankfully, there must have been at least two million of those that I had no interest in reading. I found the shelves devoted to Proust, and felt more than a little ridiculous as I surveyed the many critical studies of his writing. I had had the idea that neurology and philosophy would inform my prose contributions, and I worked hard to weave my thoughts into what I could of those discourses. But what did I really know of them, or of the France of Marcel Proust? My writing worked hard to prove itself, to earn some respect in the shadow of the overwhelming shelf. I fashioned it with a kind of fury, and I recoil now from its relentless density, its bleak persistence. These feelings must have contributed to the reasons why my part of the project lay dormant for these past ten years. I completed the first two of my three contributions—we had decided to focus on three specific parts or elements of the seven volumes; those were the beginning and the end, considered together; the long sentence that occurs at the midpoint; and a passage in which the narrator watches over the sleeping Albertine in the fifth volume. I never completed the third, despite, or maybe because of, the fact that it was in many ways the most intriguing of the three. I have a little more difficulty explaining why I have taken the opportune moment of this return to Stanford and this lecture, to awaken it. If anything this visit, and renewed proximity to the Pacific, reminds me of the profound differences between seashore and lakeshore. It also reminds me, however, of finding Jacqueline Risset's *Sleep's Powers* in the Green Library, not on the shelf of Proust studies, although not far from it, and reading in it the chapter *Sleep and the Sea,* with its considerations of Ferenczi and Thalassa as responses to the very same passage from *The Captive* that we had planned to write about. *Moreover, it was not only the sea at the close of day that existed for me in Albertine, but at times the drowsy murmur of the sea upon the shore on moonlit nights.* Rereading the sentence that starts the Proust passage, and Risset's rich scholarly associations with it, I thought of how the moon causes the tides, and the way the logic of the sea follows the double pull exerted on us at all times—the major gravity of the earth, the minor gravity of the moon.

My pole star for those days of writing was Gilles Deleuze and his volume *Proust and Signs*, one of the few Proust studies I had read. One proposal in that volume has stayed with me since then, and guided me in other ways. Deleuze's argument, stated briefly, is this: *When Proust compares his work to a cathedral or to a gown, it is not to identify himself with a Logos as a splendid totality but, on the contrary, to emphasize his right to incompletion, to seams and patches.* This captured something of the reason for my lifelong fascination with structure. The author imagines the cathedral shape of the work as a virtuality, a mathematics, and then commences to articulate it with awkward actual substances that have their own plans. The question then becomes: How far can the substance stretch the form without rupturing it? Or: How do I patch over the seam of a ten-year silence? The cathedral's doubleness for Proust posed, it seemed to me, some curious and edgy problems. The virtual cathedral, the *idea* of the cathedral, constituted the seat of its religiosity, while its actual presence, its body, in all its various exhilarating detail, engaged on the level of what Proust himself referred to as *idolatry*. The resolute refusal to transubstantiate, for body and spirit to merge, in the proximity or shadow of the transubstantiation ideal, blossomed into *hamartiology*, an ethic of inversion as fully worked out as the church's theology, attached to it like a parasite. Proust removed the architectural titles from his volumes (Porch, Apse, Window) maybe to allow this flowering of contradiction, and not to weigh the project down in the symbolic. This idea of doubleness, of two elements that resist one another within a single concept, motivated much of my writing in the first two parts of our project. For me it linked to the neurological discourse, since the workings of the brain had so often been discovered by the revelations of its misfires. These twelve years later, I might be more prone to ask *what is a cathedral* if not a vast container, *a node on an immensely complex network of economical, cultural, historical, and technological forces,* the sacred and the profane simply the two most prominent of its signatures? Now I might consider cathedral-shaped writing less as a reflection of the mind and more as a force that tempers thought and locates it. Proust wrote about his discovery of the cathedral and its transformation of his thought as he studied the writing of John Ruskin. The desire to read Ruskin began as that of accruing knowledge of, thus erudition about and enrichment by, the paintings and architecture of Europe, but the assimilation of such knowledge resulted in what we might call a sea change. Proust described it this way.

> *For Ruskin's thought is not like the thought of an Emerson, for example, which is contained in its entirety in a book, something abstract that is, a pure sign of itself. The object to which a thought like Ruskin's is applied and from which it is inseparable, is not immaterial, it is scattered across the surface of the earth. One must go to seek it wherever it is found, to Pisa, to Florence, to the National Gallery, to Rouen, to Amiens, into the mountains of Switzerland. Such a thought, which has an object other than itself, which has realized itself in space, which is thought no longer infinite and free but limited and subjugated,*

which is incarnate in bodies of sculpted marble, in snow-covered mountains, in painted faces, is perhaps less godlike than pure thought. But it makes the universe more beautiful for us, or at least certain parts of it, certain named parts, because it has touched them and initiated us into them by forcing us, if we would understand them, to love them.

Thought in this instance requires pilgrimage, to *certain named parts*. It lodges itself in the object of its quest, an object always physical. Understanding results, strangely, from the initiation of forced love. Writing becomes the *compte rendu*, the rendered account of the pilgrim and the revelations of arrival. The default condition, one might venture, is one of lack, or the desire that initiates the quest, despite the misconception of its result. At the journey's end, thought comes to rest in belief: *the intimate union of the ego with the surrounding world, felt as an absolute certainty of satisfaction, security, as well as the loss of our self to what surrounds and contains us . . .* So states Julia Kristeva in her aptly titled book *This Incredible Need to Believe*. The ecstasy of belief arises from *an exorbitant kind of more-than-life* an elation and an overflow *of this belonging of the ego to a container.* I would add that there is joy in the mis-match of self to world, the kind one might experience when trying on a garment that one aspires to wear. Kristeva mentions Proust's *dreams without images . . . woven with pleasures and/or pains that "one" "believes" (he states) unnameable, that mobilize the extreme intensity of the five senses and that only a cascade of metaphors can attempt to "translate"* . . . Such *translation,* or writing, situates the sensation, or the substance of self, in the container, or cathedral, while the *cascade of metaphors* has everything to do with the other necessary force in the life of the project—ours, not Proust's—the engine, the energy, the charge, of the voice. *I miss the voice*, my writing partner said to me as we began, as if our project could and would extend its life, bring it back. I discovered after some time that others had been so affected. Virginia Woolf wrote in a letter to Roger Fry, after reading and rereading Proust in 1922: *Proust so titillates my own desire for expression that I can hardly set out the sentence. Oh, if I could write like that! I cry. And at the moment such is the astonishing vibration and saturation and intensification that he procures—theres something sexual in it—that I feel I can write like that, and seize my pen . . .* I attribute some of this urge and impulse to write to this quality of the quest, the journey to the cathedral to find the one tiny figurine, as described by Ruskin, carved into the vast stone relief, and the way the albeit modest adventure situates thought in the world and writing as reflection, or perhaps becoming, of the journey. Thought and writing weave an apprenticeship. Something of the hypnotic identification that Virginia Woolf notes might lie here, in the way the search of the writing lends it a quality of, to borrow Calvino's term, *lightness.* I am thinking of the Kafka micro-story with which Calvino concluded his first of five lectures collected as *Six Memos for the Next Millennium:*

> *I would like to end this talk by mentioning Kafka's "Der Kübelreiter" (The Knight of the Bucket). This is a very short story written in 1917 in the first person, and its point of departure is plainly a real situation in that winter of warfare, the worst for the Austrian Empire: the lack of coal. The narrator goes out with an empty bucket to find coal for the stove. Along the way the bucket serves him as a horse, and indeed it takes him up as far as the second floor of a house where he rocks up and down as if riding on the back of a camel. The coal merchant's shop is underground, and the bucket rider is too high up. He has a hard time getting his message across to the man, who would really like to respond to his request, but the coal merchant's wife wants nothing to do with him. He begs them to give him a shovelful of even the worst coal, even though he can't pay immediately. The coal merchant's wife unties her apron and shooes away the intruder as if he were a fly. The bucket is so light that it flies off with its rider until it disappears beyond the Ice Mountains.*

Of the many things I could say about this paragraph, I might start by pointing out Calvino's curious translation of the story's title, not as *bucket rider,* but as *knight of the bucket.* I imagine the coal bucket resembles a knight's helmet, and Kafka's narrator arms himself with it as he begins his quest. The ordinary scarcity of 1917 transforms into the extraordinary lack as of a holy grail. Anything ordinary in a sense becomes extraordinary when absent. The pursuit gives the pursuer mobility, unburdened by the lightness of the empty vessel to be filled. 1917 fallsbetween the publication of Proust's first and second volumes, and the first World War of course insisted itself on the project and bent its direction considerably. The failure of Kafka's narrator to obtain his stated goal only succeeds in reinscribing the quest, as the bucket takes him instead on a flight to the very land of lack, transfigured into the Ice Mountains, their description becoming their name, as *certain named parts*. More to the point, I think, of my extensive quote of Calvino, in a consideration of thought inseparable from its material object, is the manner of Calvino's retelling of the Kafka story, as if it were more an event witnessed than literature read. Calvino relates it to his audience, and I wonder whether it has something to do with my age that I am now drawn to this sort of indirect quotation, to find something of Proust in that as well. *The most beautiful styles are the most diluted styles.* But in flying off toward the Ice Mountains, I seem to have strayed as far as possible from the stated object of my quest, the sea. So I will let Calvino make his own point:

> *It may be that Kafka only wanted to tell us that going out to look for a bit of coal on a cold wartime night changes the mere swinging of an empty bucket into the quest of a knight-errant or the desert crossing of a caravan or a flight on a magic carpet. But the idea of an empty bucket raising you above the level where one finds both the help and the egoism of others; the empty bucket, symbol of privation and desire and seeking, raising you to the point at which a humble request can no longer be satisfied—all this opens the road to endless reflection.*

One discovery that I somewhat absurdly believed I alone had made motivated me to write my part of our project, a discovery concerning the word *fugitive*. In fact, our choice of the passage describing the sleeping Albertine as the focus our third chapter, had everything to do with this single word. I recall as well that I had some idea about how the explication of this word would justify our project's continual oscillation between voices of poetry and prose. That idea has become vague to me now, or maybe it is my current voice that seems unclear beside that of the first two chapters. Another idea from Deleuze (and Guattari), this one an implicit if indirect exhortation leveled, it seemed, directly at me, might as a provenance have commanded more of my attention in those days had I allowed, as it regards *the black hole of involuntary memory as above all, something one has to get out of, escape from. Proust knows that quite well, even if his commentators do not.* I will try to reconstruct the thoughts I once had about the word *fugitive*. I will try as best I can to return to those days before I felt overcome by the burden of the unread bookshelf. I could argue that my ignorance buoyed me like the empty coal bucket. The intervening decade slipped past me in a blur of minutiae and activities intended to improve those small parts of the world I could touch. I can't explain precisely why this neglected third part has resurfaced now as a response to your generous invitation to speak at this event. Something in your three-word subject line—*work from memory*—cast me back to our Proust project. Whatever it was that we pursued with such passion, that my co-author and I imagined our work from memory would recover, finds an echo now in the almost simpleminded question of the difference between sea and lake, one of many questions that this work generated for me, or in me, questions that appeared irrelevant and useless until they became necessary. So I will say what I have to say out of gratitude—to my writing partner who finished his beautiful part on time and waited patiently for me to finish mine; to Marcel Proust of course, less an individual than a community, *of the partakers in the creative experience,* the sharable logics of creation and reception, a community we somehow thought we could know or even join from our vantage points on the edges of American mountains or lakes; and mostly to you, for framing a question, or a quest, and for listening to my report.

When the fact falls asleep it becomes a face.

One might call the sleeping face a fact but to do so would be wrong.

I recall an experience I do not know if I lived it.

At the museum, Brancusi's sleeping muse in polished bronze, sleeping in
  a stone, this complete sleeping other though only her head exists, and
  in the middle of her head, that ancient point where genius presides, a
  thumbprint.

I see I have miswritten sleeping *in* a stone when I meant to write
  sleeping *on* a stone.

I had been warned, once upon a time, by a guard, not to touch the
  bronze breast of Daphne when he saw me reaching toward it in the
  sky-lit sculpture garden with the veined marble floor; he said that the
  oil from my hand would permanently mark her breast.

He looked at me as if knew the trouble intimately.

The muse's head is polished to such a sheen it reflects back to those who
  gaze upon her their own gaze; I try not to think too much about this
  fact.

I see I have miswritten *this fact* when I meant to write *this face*.

I wonder why my own face appears so blurry in my eyes.

And then I noticed the thumbprint on the muse's head; I thought, if I
stay here forever, if I do not ever move, then my face will become dark
to me.

I might need to die for this darkness to happen but I do not know if I
need to die or only to be patient in a death-like way.

I distinctly remember in a lowered voice saying to no one at all, *she
obviously needs her rest*; I guessed in the end that I must be talking to
myself or to my reflection—I thought about my own child sleeping in
her bed in my other life long ago where perhaps she still sleeps, or so
I hope—for I found myself reaching out toward her to wake the metal
up, and as with so many things, I needed a voice to tell me that doing
so was the wrong thing to do.

Don't touch; here there is no touching; keep your hands to yourself;
these rules I have been told my entire life taught me how to work my
eyes.

The eyes work by being open.

The eyes work by being open and in this way the eyes are like the
hands.

When the eye blinks it blinks as the hand grasps when it grasps, to
   make use of the tool.

An early psychological theory posited blinking as the mind's
   apprehensive apparatus; to blink seized the image seen as a hand
   might close around a pencil to draw a portrait of the sleeping woman
   lying flower-like on my bed.

An eye cannot draw the sound of her breathing though a pencil can
   change the bed into a boat and so give a sense of her oceanic murmur
   unconscious.

The eye cannot see the sea inside us.

They did not think the eye needed to blink so as not to dry out.

They thought the eye blinked to capture the image of what is seen, and
   though the theory was abandoned as mere poetry, it led directly to
   the development of the camera, in whose dark chamber the sleeping
   woman still sleeps.

I once had a theory that the time encompassed by the eye's blinking
   exactly paralleled the span in which the eye stayed closed at night;
   but the theory was just a dream.

Now I realize that to talk to oneself is to talk to one's reflection; I
   realized this fact when I touched my own face to stop myself from
   touching hers.

I felt angry and sad; what rage was it in me that kept watch over my
thoughts as I watched the sleep of others.

To say *for many years* is not the same as saying *for as long as I can
remember*.

Time right now trespasses into vision.

For as long as I can remember, I have sat on the stairs outside my
daughter's bedroom, telling her stories as she falls asleep: the
reflection of the moon on the sea, a dropped flower floating on the
water, sound as of a ragged sail off in the distance, the sail that is the
crescent moon, pulling the earth in circles.

I would listen as my daughter became silent: a tree rooted in dreams.

Jacqueline Risset, in her miniature prose encyclopedia *Sleep's Powers*,
sees that our children need these stories to placate their awful fear that
sleep is a form of death, as if in the book resides the oldest promise
that the world will still exist when sleep ends, a promise of which
the book itself is the primary example, worlds in white pages caught
between dark covers always able to be opened again.

Then on the stairs, in the half-light of the stairs, I would open my own
book and read; sometimes it afforded me a pleasure that was less pure.

I see I have miswritten *my own book* for *the book I am reading*.

Difference becomes different when the other sleeps.

For a long time, for as long as I can remember, the narrator has no name.

My legs would fall asleep as I read on the stairs, a not unpleasant
    sensation, like an oar which one trails in the water, the current
    carrying the craft, save that the craft contains the current, as the book
    is the boat in which the tidal surge is contained, as the bed contains
    the breath in which the waves murmur and break.

The women of Malamacco and Pelestrina, as evening threatened to
    arrive, would walk to the shore and sing their shrill songs across the
    waters until they heard their husbands' voices singing in return; or so
    I read in the journal that I did not write.

Witness is a good excuse to say I.

I watched her sleep; I watched her sleep and breathe; there was a
    thumbprint on her head whose secret source filled me with jealousy,
    proof of another other me who watched her sleep in unconscious
    disregard, in intimate profile, a person who could speak to her as
    she slept, whose voice could cross the ocean and trust in her return,
    so that she might wake, her eyes fluttering beneath her lids as if
    scanning a horizon that existed only for her, seeking landmarks so
    that she would not be lost on her return, then she would find her
    tongue and say: "My—" or "My darling—" followed by my Christian
    name, which, if we give the narrator the same name as the author of
    this book, would be "My Marcel," or "My darling Marcel."

These fragments that contain the world are smaller than the world.

A name falls down the stairs that is my name, a single syllable, chirped
    as a cricket chirps its song, my wife singing down to me to return.

Yes, I turned off the light; yes, I came upstairs; yes, a glass of wine.

Is she asleep? Yes, she is asleep.

Did you peek in? Yes, I peeked in.

She was sleeping? Yes, the drowsy murmur of the sea on a moonlit night;
    Yes, the foam; Yes, the fog hovering a distance from the shore, and is
    it?, yes, it is, nearing; Yes, her eyes closed and her breathing slowed,
    her face in secret profile; Yes, a slight twitch in her fingers after she
    pushed the covers down, as if in her dream she was plucking a taut
    string to hear a peculiar note.

The song stretches for so long across the sea I grow drowsy
    remembering it.

I confess, I have spent much of my adult life pondering the intricacies
    of likeness and unlikeness, coming to few conclusions, trusting and
    mistrusting that the curve of a wave and the curve of the crescent
    moon, or that tears and sea-water, wake each in the other as I wake
    each morning in myself; as I wake up again as myself in myself half-
    trusting; and then I live my day, reading books, writing a line or

two, maybe a paragraph in which I walk along the shore along the line where the sand is dark and light where the waves roll back, a paragraph I might later emend, where I am walking on the shore and the sun sits on the horizon for such a long time it no longer seems to be the sun, but a plate on a mantel catching the bronze light from the other room.

Because I don't own enough bookshelves these books are double-stacked and bend the wooden slat; one row sits in front of another, hiding those other titles behind the display of their own.

I've read many of these books, perhaps most of them, but I remember very little of them; for many hours I've pored over these pages, marking thoughts in the margins, entering my own thoughts into another's thoughts as might a hopeful or mistrustful lover, asking questions as if but nonchalant asides responding to something you just said, just then, a moment ago, as you tie the sash of your robe around your waist, a comment about an old friend, something she said once, a very witty something said, but you can't remember who said it, you only remember laughing and spilling your glass of wine whose claret edge spilled across the white tablecloth as a wave that never recedes until its whole volume is spent, a question to pry out secrets, the secrets hidden in the words, but what my question was, written in pencil, in the margin, in my illegible scrawl, I cannot remember; I can hardly remember what it was those books were telling me.

I do remember a rose-bush growing on the edge of a cliff overlooking the sea, and a butterfly deep in a bloom; on the horizon a sailing ship seemed to move slowly from one flower to a next, a distance the butterfly crossed with but a few beats of her wings, while for the ship it took hours; I remember I wrote next to the passage *love collapses subjective distances into a single span*; but that page is hidden in a book hidden behind another book so that my own thought is a rumor I tell to myself.

I see I have been speaking again about books when I meant to speak about the ocean.

I see I have been speaking again about oceans when I meant to speak about sleep.

I see I keep saying *you* when I mean to say *she*, and say *yours* when I mean to say *hers*.

On top of the book shelf where, if one should think of the volumes below it as celestial bodies—each book a star, some brighter in the firmament than others, and my thinking about them the ancient navigator's impulse to draw lines between those stars, lines that keep the sailor at night from losing his way but the same lines that tell him stories, so that to know where one is located in the blank vast of the night-ocean is also to know what stories you're being told, it is to hear the singing strung in lines across the tuning-key stars—on the top of the book shelf lay Gilles Deleuze's volume *Proust and Signs*, given to me by my distinguished colleague before I left the city in which we both lived, a book he hoped would help me as we began our collaboration on *In Search of Lost Time*, a work we discovered we both loved as we talked over coffee one afternoon; I worked diligently for a time, for years, but for years have done nothing; nor have I read the book he gave me, the book, that were the volumes below it celestial bodies, would be the pole star; but it is not a North I have found.

A closed book announces its name, but it is not beholden to it; it has its
name written on its face; it has its name written on its spine. I have,
in more unbalanced moments in my life, suspected that behind the
face every page is blank, and in what felt to me a jealous fit I would
open a book as quickly as I could to catch it in its blankness, in its
being only for itself, but I never succeeded; sometimes, when opening
a book of poetry the breadth of white space would for an instant fool
me, and then I would feel as if had been chosen, as a hero-wanderer
of old, to enter into a different realm, life's other order, to witness the
world that refuses words; and then I would see a word and that other
world would depart back into its rich silence; once, those words that
dispelled me were *she grew calm again in the sleep / from which she had
not emerged.*

A book often read, or read once furiously, placed on a table on its spine,
will open to a page, a page I call crisis.

Crisis is a form of jealousy in which one wants to be the envied other.

Jealousy is the impossible sense of being the other you envy, a sense in
which you realize yourself as the shadow of another self, a shadow
whose motions seem freely chosen but are not, though the thoughts
that arise from these motions—brushing her hair behind her ear as
she turns away from you in the bedroom—are all terribly one's own.

When I put the book on the table, when I let it open to where it would
open—repeating for myself an old magic, an old reading of fate—I
learned many things I already knew but which I had forgotten; such
is the nature of fate: the amnesiac remembering his name when a
stranger calls him by name, and hearing his name, remembering that

Marcel is me myself, realizing the stranger is no stranger at all, but is she who I love; I remembered that on either side of the broken spine the pages curl as waves curl; I remembered that the sleeping book when opened becomes an ocean dividing itself in two, each page a wave rolling away from the other to margins none can see, and the middle of the book, that chasm from which the waves in opposite directions run, is where Charybdis hides, swallowing the blank water, creating whirlpools, threatening the reader's little craft, mocking it, saying it will not hold, meaning and words, it will not hold.

I am a leaky craft.

And when I remembered my name, I mean to say, when I remembered the open book was the sleeping, sleepless ocean, I remembered each word contained some portion of breath, my breath or another's breath I do not know, nor does it matter, as the air, like the water, is in common; it is a common sort of craft: breathing, words.

There the ocean heaved, there on my table; *As I continued to hear, to capture from moment to moment, the murmur, soothing as a barely perceptible breeze, of her pure breath, it was a whole physiological existence that was spread out before me, at my disposal; just as I used to remain for hours lying on the beach, in the moonlight, so long could I have remained there gazing at her, listening to her. Sometimes it was as though the sea was beginning to swell, as though the storm was making itself felt even inside the bay, and I would press myself against her and listen to the gathering roar of her breath.*

It is true, those rumors; if you put your ear close to the page you will hear the ocean breathing.

That rumor, the one I told you yesterday, the same one told to me many
   years ago (by whom I forget), that her face is an ocean—

I mean that the ocean is her face—

I mean that rumor that her face is in the book which is an ocean—

I mean that rumor that she has a face through which she breathes—

That rumor that she breathes underwater—

That rumor that the ocean is composed of breath—

I am writing you this letter, my distinguished colleague, to say to you
   that this rumor is a fact.

(The muse blushes when she runs away.)

I am writing to say that the rumor is true.

*T*ime's flying by, time we'll never know again,
while we in our delighted state savoured our subject bit by bit.

Roughly two-thirds of the way through the third and last book of *The Georgics*, Virgil offers this wake-up call transition, translated here by Peter Fallon. Virgil recalibrates the stakes of the discourse, in this case the care of livestock, now that the horizon of the end of the poem has appeared. Bach might call this strategy of sudden acceleration a *terraced dynamic,* a discontinuous leap from slow to quick. Virgil's words suggest a slippage between our time, the slowness of our savoring the subject, and time itself, of the universe or the day, which impels us to an end of a different and indifferent sort. The first line in the original Latin reads as follows:

Sed fugit interea, fugit irreparabile tempus

However flight meanwhile, flight irreparable of time

Irreparabile also translates as that which cannot be restored or renewed, purchased, or obtained in exchange; that which has been lost.

A true scholar, it seemed to me, could make a strong case that these lines from *The Georgics* inspired the title, *In Search of Lost Time*, as well as that of the work's final volume, published in 1927, *Le Temps retrouvé. Retrouvé* means *found* after all, or retrieved. The lost and found of the search, so the argument would run, was sensibly watched over by the great tour guide, Virgil. The word *fugit* might also come into play in this archeology. It after all provides the root for the penultimate title *The Fugitive.* The echo of the word, directly from Virgil and indirectly across the other titles, would raise the question: Who flies in *The Fugitive,* and how precisely does this flight echo time's?

I lacked the time and scholarship to prove the point, or to find where someone had already proven it, and so the matter rested. The unproven theory became my imaginary cathedral, the perfectly formed container that would one day house all my scattered thoughts and crystallize them to lucid harmony. I dreamed about the writing of it. My actual writing sometimes skirted its edges, or even rendered this or that of its fragmentary artifacts with a kind of clarity, but the dream, and the writing, slipped repeatedly into the same memory as abject digression. I'm back in high school in Michigan, my freshman year, and I have landed the position of Stage Manager in the spring musical production of *The Sound of Music*. It's my first serious entry into the theater. Through the weeks of rehearsal, the small army of bit actors doubling as crew have come to accept my authority, and I have mobilized them to change the scene behind the curtain in time with the student orchestra's interlude. Silently and in semi-darkness, they enact their invisible choreography of relocating furniture, objects, step units, and vacate the stage in time for the curtains to open. As the banks of light, operated by my classmate Steve Wilson, son of the basketball coach (who knew he had this talent?), behind the audience in his little booth, flood our work and animate the disparate parts into an opulent ballroom in Salzburg circa 1939, I stand in the wings and watch the actors enter, and feel the strange and palpable sensation of the audience drifting into a dream. They seem to conspire with the Von Trapp family to take flight across the mountains, as the student actors (their own children, in some cases) speak the first words of the scene. I cannot follow their travels, but can facilitate them. I can oversee the engineering of their escape.

The search begins with sleep. The writer dreams of the book as a life. It ends with the book rediscovered, or retrieved. Now sleep and a book define its counterpoint as well, its furthest limit, the waves at the edge of its perception. The narrator goes to *fetch a book from my father's study* and returns to find Albertine asleep, her breathing inducing his extended contemplation of the ocean surf on a moonlit night. It is the other who flies like time, her breath like nature's metronome of waves. She has been the subject of an experiment of forced love, a tragedy that has absorbed the narrator more deeply into the world. Now she sleeps, and as she sleeps she travels to immaterial lands he cannot know. He watches her slow breathing, and imagines the speed of her sleep. He stands in attendance over her as she flies away to unnamed parts, and here he even gives his own name—*My darling Marcel* she will say upon waking. What does this "in attendance over" mean? Only this: the drawing of a likeness between those observable surfaces, of her and some material resonance: breath, waves. This is the humble fruit of the labor of locating thought in the world. This likeness is the only harvest, the restoration of the lost, or better, the marking of the constant oscillation between loss and restoration as two amplitudes of flight. Such marking is the nature of the search; the constant making of the self and the world in flight. But here the writer plays another role. Albertine can sleep differently, safely perhaps, knowing that he is there, awake and watchful. His guardian wakefulness allows her sleep, even as he reads her as he does a book. I will remember him, and leave him that way: vigilant, reading.

The erotic suspicion:
every surface hides
a depth. Blank
page, sleeping face;
a poem's logic
stricter than logician's
logic—a logic
not lacking desire.
If consummates then.

If irreparable, time
is *then* location—
not a simple
rhyming *when*. When

a child I
read many books,
I read many
books, I read
many books. These
damaged me with
my own wanting.

In some pages
I'm captive still,
asleep in white
sheets. Words hold
their breath; words
see so quietly
they never wake
me from my

dream: a woman
puts her hand
to her breast
as she sleeps
in my bed

(this dream occurs
in anapests)

and I wanting
watch her. I
like to think
she's dreaming of
me in my
dream, this dream
the book has
given me, this
dream that does
not cease. Of
waking, there is
none. Before bed
each night I
read my book,
I read my
book, I read
my book, and

when I fall
asleep I do
not know I
fall asleep. In
my sleep I
am still reading
my book. It

watches me as
I read it;
it sees me
as in it
I sleep the
sleep it gives
me, as in
it I dream
the dream that
is the book

is the book
in which I
sleep and dream.

NOTES AND SOURCES

PAGE 2

"The neurology team's report introduces the patient KC post-accident . . . ": Rosenbaum, R. Shayna, *et al.*, "Visual imagery deficits, impaired strategic retrieval, or memory loss: disentangling the nature of an amnesic person's autobiographical memory deficit." *Neuropsychologia* 42 (2004): 1619–1635. I have tried to represent the research accurately while fictionalizing some of the anecdotal details. The italicized passage is a direct quote from this report's introduction, omitting only the citations of the individual authors.

PAGE 4

"The research of Nicola Clayton . . . ": Zimmer, Carl, "Time in the Animal Mind." *The New York Times* 3 April 2007. (This article also discusses KC above.) Eaton, Joe, "Wild Neighbors: Thinking About Breakfast: The Mind of the Jay Revisited." *Berkeley Daily Planet,* 20 March 2007.

PAGE 6

"*Sometimes, my candle scarcely out, my eyes would close so quickly that I did not have time to say to myself: 'I'm falling asleep.'*": Proust, Marcel. *The Way By Swann's*. Trans. Lydia Davis. London: Penguin Books, 2003, 7.

"*. . . it seemed to me that I myself was the immediate subject of the book: a church, a quartet, the rivalry between Francois I and Charles V . . .*": Proust, Marcel. *Swann's Way*. Trans. C.K. Scott Moncrieff and Terence Kilmartin; revised by D.J. Enright. New York: The Modern Library, 1998, 1.

"*This belief lived on for a few seconds . . .*" and "*I would ask myself what time it might be . . .*": Davis translation, 7.

PAGE 8

"*As I entered the library where I had been pursuing this train of thought . . .*": Proust, Marcel. *Time Regained*. Trans. C.K. Scott Moncrieff and Terence Kilmartin; revised by D.J. Enright. New York: The Modern Library, 1999, 281 and 283.

the intelligence always comes after: Italicized lines in this paragraph derive from *Proust and Signs* by Gilles Deleuze, the critical work that perhaps most clearly comprehends how memory cannot cohere as a singular subject. "There is no Logos; there are only hieroglyphs," Deleuze states, emphatically pinpointing one of many differences between Proust and Socrates. ". . . the Socratic demon, irony, consists in anticipating the encounters. In Socrates, the intelligence still comes before the encounters; it provokes them, it instigates and organizes them." For Proust, however, to think is to observe, interpret and translate—the contents, shape, and event of the encounter. Deleuze, Gilles. *Proust and Signs*. Trans. R. Howard. Minneapolis: University of Minnesota Press, 2000, 101–102.

". . . *the tendency of the brain to integrate signals with whatever interactions are available to it*": "**Closure; filling-in.** The tendency of the brain to integrate signals with whatever interactions are available to it. Filling-in is found in the failure to notice the blind spot; other examples include cases of denial such as those found in **anosognosia.**" Edelman, Gerald. *Wider Than the Sky*. New Haven: Yale University Press, 2004, 153.

"*I saw everything reel, as one does when one falls from a horse . . .*": Proust, Marcel. *Within a Budding Grove*. Trans. C.K. Scott Moncrieff and Terence Kilmartin; revised by D.J. Enright. New York: The Modern Library, 1998, 98–99.

"*. . . are at once the thing to be translated and the translation itself*.": "The essences are at once the thing to be translated and the translation itself, the sign and the meaning." Deleuze, *Proust and Signs*, 101–102.

"The traumatic by definition resists absorption, obstructs time's flow and transformation into a life": In his review of the misguided repair demonstrated by Albert Feuillerat's volume on Proust, Samuel Beckett allows two concessions. Here is the first.

> The original edition of *A le Recherche du Temps Perdu*, as undertaken by Grasset in 1913, was to consist of three volumes, *Du Côté de Chez Swann*, *Le Côté de Guermantes* and *Le Temps Retrouvé*, or about 1,500 pages. This edition, when the first volume only had appeared, was interrupted by the War. The current edition, complete by the N.R.F. in 1924, consists of 16 volumes or about 4,000 pages.

After summarizing Feuillerat's research, Beckett offers the second concession: "The revealed Proust is no less than trine."

Beckett then challenges Feuillerat's assertion that had Proust lived longer he would have labored toward "Uniformity, homogeneity, cohesion, selection scavenging for verisimilitude (the stock-in-trade exactly of the naturalism that Proust abominated) . . ."

It is my claim, not Beckett's, of linkage between these three ideas—the rupture of trauma (the War), the self in discrete parts, and the purposeful disuniting of those parts as a form of creativity. I would hope to characterize the difference not as a disagreement, but in the absence of Beckett, who can say? I have considered the following sentence, toward the end of his tiny significant essay, of supreme importance.

> The book is the search, stated in the full complexity of all its clues and blind alleys, for that resolution, and not the *compte rendu* after the event, of a round trip.

Beckett, Samuel. "Proust in Pieces." *Disjecta*. New York: Grove Press, 1984, 63–65.

"[. . . *in Proust*] *there is no longer really any subject, but only—with singular materialism—an infinite drifting and a casual colliding of objects and sensations . . .*": Agamben, Giorgio. *Infancy and History—On the Destruction of Experience*. Trans. Liz Heron. London and New York: Verso, 2007, 49.

How strange to confuse abundance with lack, to subordinate subject to unity. Agamben's facile assertion of an absent subject in Proust falls into a familiar trap of thought: that of presuming a subject singular, and upon observing it to be multiple, concluding that it is nonexistent. Bergson (Deleuze's Bergson) referred to this as the problem of the more mistaken for the less.

> His [Bergson's] analyses [. . .] are famous. [. . .] they consist of showing that there is not *less*, but *more* in the idea of nonbeing than that of being, in disorder than in order, in the possible than in the real. In the idea of nonbeing there is in fact the idea of being, plus a logical operation of generalized negation, plus the particular psychological motive for that operation (such as when a being does not correspond to our expectation and we grasp it purely as a lack, the absence of what interests us).

Deleuze, Gilles. *Bergsonism*. Trans. Hugh Tomlinson and Barbara Habberjam. New York: Zone Books, 1991, 17.

Beckett refers to the individual in Proust as "a succession of individuals": "Breathing is habit. Life is habit. Or rather life is a succession of habits, since the individual is a succession of individuals . . . " Beckett, Samuel. *Proust*. New York: Grove Press, 1957, 8.

Gerald Edelman describes an analogous error in neurology: that of the imaginary executive, the one we produce because we cannot grasp the reality of a brain made up of independent parts that synchronize with no single authority to guide them. This "binding problem" tempts us to imagine an executive as presence rather than as function, as a brain part rather than pattern. He likens the mysterious synchronization of the brain population that results from reentrant pathways of neuronal firing to the image of musicians playing perfectly with no conductor.

> A net effect of this reentrant traffic is the time-locked or synchronized firing of neuronal groups in particular circuits. This provides the coordination in time and space that would otherwise have to be assured by some form of computation. To help imagine how reentry works, consider a hypothetical string quartet made up of willful musicians. Each plays his or her own tune with different rhythm. Now

connect the bodies of all the players with very fine threads (many of them to all body parts). As each player moves, he or she will unconsciously send waves of movement to the others. In a short time, the rhythm and to some extent the melodies will become more coherent. The dynamics will continue, leading to a new coherent output.
Edelman, Gerald. *Second Nature—Brain Science and Human Knowledge*. New Haven and London: Yale University Press, 2006, 30.

Beckett proposes that Proust's "succession of individuals" cohere into a self or subject as a "retrospective hypothesis" or only after the fact, as one looks back on one's life: "But the poisonous ingenuity of Time in the science of affliction is not limited to its action on the subject, that action, as has been shown, resulting in an unceasing modification of his personality, whose permanent reality, if any, can only be apprehended as a retrospective hypothesis." Beckett, *Proust*, 4.

Beckett's phrase uncannily parallels that of T. H. Huxley, "retrospective prophecy," as cited by Edelman (67) as a description of the proof of neurological truth. Huxley, T.H. "On the Method of Zadig: Retrospective Prophecy as a Function of Science." *Science and Hebrew Tradition: Essays by Thomas H. Huxley*. New York: Appleton, 1894, 1–22.

PAGE 14

"How can we understand the encounter between *two separate and immanent dynamisms related by no system of synchronization?*": "The observer infects the observed with his own mobility. Moreover, when it is the case of human intercourse, we are faced by the problem of an object whose mobility is not merely a function of the subject's, but independent and personal: two separate and immanent dynamisms related by no system of synchronisation." Beckett, *Proust*, 6–7.

"One could recognize the steeple of Saint-Hilaire from quite far off inscribing its unforgettable form on the horizon where Combray had not yet appeared": Proust, *The Way by Swann's*, Davis translation, 65. Both the Davis and the Moncrieff/Kilmartin translations of this passage use the word *unforgettable*.

"We may note the orienting spire of the Saint-Hilaire church in Combray as the quintessential *landmark* with respect to the five guiding elements of environment imageability and wayfinding: path, edge, district, node, and landmark": Lynch, Kevin. *The Image of the City*. Cambridge, Mass.: Massachusetts Institute of Technology, 1960. Lynch identifies and names the five elements of an environment, and on page 128 discusses the steeple in Combray as both physical landmark and conspicuous "apparition" of memory.

PAGE 16

"When I was a boy living in Germany . . . ": Carroll, James. "War's Sacred Toll," *The Boston Globe* 18 June 2007.

PAGE 18

"Combray was simply a small town like hundreds of others." Proust, Marcel. *Time Regained*. Trans. Andreas Mayor and Terence Kilmartin. New York: The Modern Library, 153–4.

PAGE 22

"miracle of the courtyard": Beckett, *Proust*, 53.

PAGE 24

"but by virtue of its bigness": "Beyond a certain critical mass, a building becomes a Big Building. Such a mass can no longer be controlled by a single architectural gesture, or even by any combination of architectural gestures. This impossibility triggers the autonomy of its parts, but that is not the same as fragmentation: the parts remain committed to the whole." Koolhaas, Rem. "Bigness or the problem of Large." *SMLXL*. New York: The Monacelli Press, 1995, 499–500.

PAGE 26

"the obliteration (regaining) of time": "Time is not recovered, it is obliterated." Beckett, *Proust*, 56.

PART 2: THE LONG SENTENCE

POETRY NOTE

The poems comprising "The Long Sentence (II)" use Proust's infamous long sentence as the source/limit for all their language. Not an erasure, but a gleaning, the poems were composed by first reading forward through the sentence, and then reading backward through the sentence—this process repeated as many times as there are poems.

PROSE NOTES AND SOURCES

Quotations appear in italics. Proust, Marcel. *Sodom and Gomorrah*. Trans. John Sturrock. London: Penguin Books, 2004. Uncredited quotes, and the long sentence word count, derive from this translation.

PAGE 33

Deleuze, Gilles. *Proust and Signs*. Trans. R. Howard. Minneapolis: University of Minnesota Press, 2000.

The mystery in Proust is the mystery of the other: Levinas, Emmanuel. "The Other in Proust." *The Levinas Reader*, Ed. S. Hand. Oxford and Cambridge: Blackwell, 1989, 163.

PAGE 35

Sacks, Oliver. "In the Moment: Music and Amnesia." *Musicophilia*. New York: Vintage, Random House, 2008.

PAGE 37

Llinás, Adolpho R. *I of the Vortex—from Neurons to Self*. Cambridge, MA: The MIT Press, 2001.

PAGE 39

Kairos and the Sophists: Barthes, Roland. *The Neutral*. Trans. R. E. Krauss and D. Hollier. New York: Columbia University Press, 2005, 169.

PAGE 41

. . . the movement by which reality exceeds its definition . . . : Levinas, *The Other in Proust*. 162.

PAGE 43

Proust life/work diagram: Barthes, *The Neutral*, 142.

PAGE 45

I found out about language [. . .] made up of unemotional sentences: Stein, Gertrude. "Plays." *Lectures in America*. London: Virago Press, 1988, 93.

PAGE 49

. . . the silver coffeepot [. . .] opposite rue d'Anjou: Albaret, Céleste. *Monsieur Proust*. Trans. Barbara Bray, New York, St. Louis, San Francisco, Toronto: McGraw-Hill, 1976, 71.

PAGE 51

. . . the very structure of appearances which are both what they are and the infinity of what they exclude . . . : Levinas, *The Other in Proust*, 162.

PART 3: WORK FROM MEMORY

POETRY NOTES

The "journal I did not write" is that of Henry David Thoreau, specifically here, March 14, 1838. Please note that some sections interweave themselves with language pulled directly from *The Captive*, pages 83–91, cited below. Sometimes these are italicized, but not always.

PROSE NOTES AND SOURCES

Moreover, it was not only the sea at the close of day [. . .] As quickly as she had earlier fallen asleep, she had awoken: Proust, Marcel. *The Captive*. Trans. C.K. Scott Moncrieff and Terence Kilmartin; revised by D.J. Enright. New York: The Modern Library, 1999, 83–91.

. . . old clothes upon old sticks to scare a bird . . . : "Among School Children" by William Butler Yeats.

Risset, Jacqueline. *Sleep's Powers*. Trans. Jennifer Moxley. Brooklyn, New York: Ugly Duckling Presse, 2008, 25.

Ferenczi, Sándor. "Thalassa—A Theory of Genitality." *The Psychoanalytic Quarterly*. 1938. London: H. Karnac (Books) Ltd, 1989, 2.

When Proust compares his work to a cathedral or to a gown . . . : Deleuze, *Proust and Signs*, 161.

Proust removed the architectural titles from his volumes (Porch, Apse, Window): Olson, Liesl. *Modernism and the Ordinary*. Oxford: Oxford University Press, 2009, 48.

"a node on an immensely complex network of economical, cultural, historical, and technological forces": Powers, Richard. "Making the Rounds." *Intersections*, Ed. Stephen Burn and Peter Dempsey. Urbana–Champaign, Illinois: Dalkey Archive Press, 2008, 305–306.

For Ruskin's thought is not like the thought of an Emerson . . . : Proust, Marcel. "John Ruskin." Trans. John Sturrock. *Days of Reading*, Penguin, London, 2008, 40–41. Kristeva, Julia. *This Incredible Need to Believe*. Trans. Beverley Bie Brahic. New York: Columbia University Press, 2009, 7, 35.

Virginia Woolf wrote in a letter to Roger Fry . . . . : Olson, *Modernism and the Ordinary*, 168–169.

Calvino, Italo. "Lightness." *Six Memos for the Next Millennium*. Cambridge, Massachusetts: Harvard University Press, 1988, 27–28.

The most beautiful styles are the most diluted styles: Lin, Tan. *BlipSoak01*. Berkeley, California: Atelos, 2003, 11.

Gilles Deleuze and Felix Guattari, *A Thousand Plateaus: Capitalism and Schizophrenia*, tr. B. Massumi, page 186, Universtiy of Minnesota Press, Minneapolis, 1987.

The Georgics of Virgil. Trans. Peter Fallon. Loughcrew, Ireland: The Gallery Press, 2004, 78.

ACKNOWLEDGMENTS

The authors would like to thank the editors of the following journals for kindly publishing sections of *Work from Memory*: *Black Warrior Review, The Denver Quarterly, New Orleans Review,* and *Octopus.*

The graphic on page 43 is from *The Neutral* by Roland Barthes. Copyright © 2005 Columbia University Press. Reprinted with permission of the publisher.

The image on the rear cover is *Daguerreotype 4: Architectural study taken in Italy, almost certainly Venice,* by John Ruskin (1819–1900), 1840s. Copyright © Museum of the History of Science, Oxford.

DAN BEACHY-QUICK is the author of five books of poetry, most recently *Circle's Apprentice,* as well as a number of chapbooks, including *Apology for the Book of Creatures.* He has also collaborated with the poet Srikanth Reddy on *Conversities.* Works of prose—essays, meditation, and tales—include *A Whaler's Dictionary* and *Wonderful Investigations.* His work has been supported by the Lannan Foundation. He teaches in the MFA Writing Program at Colorado State University.

MATTHEW GOULISH co-founded the performance groups Goat Island (in 1987) and *Every house has a door* (in 2008). His *39 Microlectures—in proximity of performance* was published by Routledge in 2000, and *Small Acts of Repair—Performance, Ecology, and Goat Island,* which he co-edited with Stephen Bottoms, in 2007. *The Brightest Thing in the World—3 Lectures from The Institute of Failure* was published in an edition of 500 by Green Lantern Press, 2012. He was awarded a Lannan Foundation Writers Residency in 2004, and in 2007 he received an honorary Ph.D. from Dartington College of Arts, University of Plymouth. Goulish teaches in the MFA and BFA Writing Programs of The School of the Art Institute of Chicago.

AHSAHTA PRESS

SAWTOOTH POETRY PRIZE SERIES

2002: Aaron McCollough, *Welkin* (Brenda Hillman, judge)

2003: Graham Foust, *Leave the Room to Itself* (Joe Wenderoth, judge)

2004: Noah Eli Gordon, *The Area of Sound Called the Subtone* (Claudia Rankine, judge)

2005: Karla Kelsey, *Knowledge, Forms, The Aviary* (Carolyn Forché, judge)

2006: Paige Ackerson-Kiely, *In No One's Land* (D. A. Powell, judge)

2007: Rusty Morrison, *the true keeps calm biding its story* (Peter Gizzi, judge)

2008: Barbara Maloutas, *the whole Marie* (C. D. Wright, judge)

2009: Julie Carr, *100 Notes on Violence* (Rae Armantrout, judge)

2010: James Meetze, *Dayglo* (Terrance Hayes, judge)

2011: Karen Rigby, *Chinoiserie* (Paul Hoover, judge)

AHSAHTA PRESS

NEW SERIES

This book is set in Apollo MT type
with Scala Sans Bold titles
by Ahsahta Press at Boise State University.
Cover design by Quemadura.
Book design by Janet Holmes.
Printed in Canada.

AHSAHTA PRESS

2012

JANET HOLMES, DIRECTOR

CHRISTOPHER CARUSO

JODI CHILSON

KYLE CRAWFORD

CHARLES GABEL

JESSICA HAMBLETON, *intern*

RYAN HOLMAN

MELISSA HUGHES, *intern*

TORIN JENSEN

ANNIE KNOWLES

STEPHA PETERS

JULIE STRAND